Praise for *Amp It Up*

"In my 30+ year experience as a venture investor I have never seen anyone rival Frank's operating know-how. With Frank, it all starts and ends with hardcore and focused execution. 'Get comfortable with being uncomfortable', 'hope is not a strategy', and 'the best way to build a brand is to get more customers' are some of the mantras by which Frank has taught us to live. There is no doubt that he has made many of us better board members, as we assist other CEOs along their journeys."

—Doug Leone,
Partner, Sequoia Capital

"Frank Slootman is one of the best performing CEOs there is. This book is essential reading for every leader who aspires to motivate teams, inspire excellence, and deliver beyond expectations."

—Bill McDermott,
President and CEO, ServiceNow

"*Amp It Up* is a terrific read for leaders and future leaders, whether they are at a start-up, an SMB, or a big company. As a CEO, Frank exudes total clarity on what to do, and equally as important what not to do. . . so if you are looking for a must-read about leadership, being focused on your mission, and executing at the highest levels, this is the book!"

—Joe Tucci,
former Chairman and CEO, EMC

"Over the past 15 years, I've had a front-row seat to watch Frank Slootman's operational excellence on display at Data Domain, ServiceNow, and Snowflake. What makes Frank the best technology CEO on the planet: he sets and then beats unreasonably high expectations; he is a high-integrity people leader; he makes the strategy clear to all; and he is a fearless leader willing to do whatever it takes to win. *Amp It Up* is a must-read book for anyone looking to take their team and organization to the next level."

—Mike Speiser,
Managing Director, Sutter Hill Ventures

"Frank worked for me as Data Domain became EMC and – wow! – what an incredible leader. He built an intensity around clear business priorities and the customer value proposition and drove it through the organization daily. *Amp It Up* tells that story and how it can be recreated in other organizations."

—Pat Gelsinger,
CEO, Intel

"Frank Slootman brings his experience of delivering success into plain sight for all of us to learn and be inspired by: simplify the value proposition, focus on the customer, take away distraction and confusion, relentlessly drive execution with excellence, faster. . . *Amp It Up* is a recipe we can all apply."

—**Frans van Houten,**
CEO of Royal Philips

AMP
IT
UP

FRANK SLOOTMAN

AMP IT UP

Leading for Hypergrowth by Raising Expectations, Increasing Urgency, and Elevating Intensity

WILEY

Library of Congress Cataloging-in-Publication Data is Available:

ISBN 9781119836117 (Hardback)
ISBN 9781119836407 (ePDF)
ISBN 9781119836414 (ePub)

Cover Design: Wiley/Kathy Davis
Cover Image: ©Irina Karpinchik/Getty Images

SKY10091843_112224

To the Man (and Woman) in the Arena:

*"It is not the critic who counts; not the man who points out
how the strong man stumbles, or where the doer of deeds could
have done them better. The credit belongs to the man who is actually in
the arena, whose face is marred by dust and sweat and blood;
who strives valiantly; who errs, who comes short again and again,
because there is no effort without error and shortcoming;
but who does actually strive to do the deeds; who knows great
enthusiasms, the great devotions; who spends himself in a worthy
cause; who at the best knows in the end the triumph of high
achievement, and who at the worst, if he fails, at least fails while
daring greatly, so that his place shall never be with those cold and
timid souls who neither know victory nor defeat."*

—Theodore Roosevelt, 1910

Contents

PART

I

Amping Up

1

Introduction: The Power of Amping Up

Amp It Up

A few years ago I wrote a popular LinkedIn article, "Amp It Up," whose main premise was that organizations have considerable room to improve their performance *without* making expensive changes to their talent, structure, or fundamental business model. My basic advice was to keep playing your game but amp things up dramatically. Raise your standards, pick up the pace, sharpen your focus, and align your people. You don't need to bring in reams of consultants to examine everything that is going on. What you need on day one is to ratchet up expectations, energy, urgency, and intensity.

That article triggered thousands of likes, shares, and comments. It also led to a flood of incoming requests for sit-downs and speaking engagements. While I love speaking to other leaders, especially entrepreneurs, and while I speak at conferences and business schools from time to time, I couldn't possibly accommodate everyone who wanted to learn more about my Amp It Up philosophy. I believe it's incumbent on leaders to share our experience with others, but doing so in small groups (let alone one-on-one) isn't efficient or scalable, especially when you have a consuming day job. That's why I'm writing this book: to summarize my convictions, observations, and beliefs about how to lead a mission-driven, high-performance company.

The concepts, strategies, and tactics you will find here were developed over my entire career but especially at the three very different companies where I served as CEO: Data Domain from 2003 to 2010, ServiceNow from 2011 to 2017, and Snowflake from 2019 to the present. At various times I've also been a venture capitalist, a board member, and a corporate executive, but no experience in business compares to being CEO. I love being fully accountable for a company's leadership, strategy, culture, and execution in an ultra-competitive marketplace.

Things can go bad very quickly in an organization when the leadership team is weak or gets distracted. Human nature being what it is, many people will slow their output to a glacial pace and adopt "good enough" as their standard. Without focused leadership, millions of conflicting priorities compete with each other. Then the best people in the organization get frustrated and start to leave, as talent and energy go untapped and dormant. At this point you're on the path to catastrophic decline—unless you amp things up immediately.

Leadership changes can yield immediate impact long before you can carry out more structural changes in talent, organization, and strategy. You can engulf your organization with energy, step up the tempo, and start executing the basic blocking and tackling with a lot more focus and higher expectations. It will feel like busting a log jam. All of a sudden, everything is moving and shaking.

This phenomenon is not limited to business. We often see sports teams go from losing to winning from one season to the next without dramatic changes in roster. When Vince Lombardi took over as head coach of the Green Bay Packers in 1959, the team had just come off a 1–10 season, not to mention 11 losing seasons in row. The next year, the Packers improved to 7–5, their first winning season in many years. Then they started winning one division championship after another. Leadership really matters. It's no coincidence that to this day, winners of the Super Bowl receive a trophy named for Lombardi.

My goal for this book is to provide not merely tactical advice but also context and ways of thinking about situations. You can try these ideas on for size and see if they fit. I'm not on a mission to convince the world to agree with me. If you choose not to amp it up, that's up to you. But I believe the chapters ahead will help you stiffen your spine and fight the good fight—not just if you're a CEO but if you're a leader at any level, whether at a start-up, a big company, or a nonprofit.

I also believe that you can only get these insights from a fellow traveler. No offense to my VC friends, but they often think that their investments give them the right to lecture entrepreneurs at board meetings, even though many VCs have never been in the combat seat themselves. Having seen things done is not the same as doing them.

The media have praised the results that my three companies have delivered over the past two decades, as we ramped up to three successful IPOs and generated hundreds of billions of dollars in market value. It's hard to argue with results. But outsiders have also questioned, if not criticized, the ways in which we achieved those results. So let's start with an overview of the five key steps in the Amp It Up process: raise your standards, align your people, sharpen your focus, pick up the pace, and transform your strategy.

Raise Your Standards

The late Steve Jobs was only inspired by "insanely great" things. He set a high bar for seemingly everything, and anything that didn't meet his standards was summarily rejected. Try applying "insanely great" as a standard on a daily basis and see how far you get. People lower their standards in an effort to move things along and get things off their desks. Don't do it. Fight that impulse every step of the way. It doesn't take much more mental energy to raise standards. Don't let malaise set in. Bust it up. Raising the bar is energizing by itself.

Instead of telling people what I think of a proposal, a product, a feature, whatever, I ask them instead what they think. Were they thrilled with it? Absolutely love it? Most of the time I would hear, "It's okay," or "It's not bad." They would surmise from my facial expression that this wasn't the answer I was looking for. Come back when *you* are bursting with excitement about whatever you are proposing to the rest of us.

We should all be thrilled with what we're doing. So channel your inner Steve Jobs. Aim for insanely great. It's much more energizing!

Align Your People and Culture

Alignment becomes a more important concept as a business grows and there are many moving parts. The question is, are we all pulling on the same oar? Are we all driving in the same direction?

When I joined Snowflake, the company was being run as what I would call a pseudo-SaaS company with a subscription model.

But it's basically a utility company for cloud computing with a consumption model. As with your local electric company, you pay only for what you use. Yet, like a SaaS company, our sales force was completely focused on bookings, or sales contract value, even though Snowflake did not recognize a single revenue dollar on bookings. Only actual consumption causes revenue to be recognized. Consumption drove bookings only indirectly; as customers ran out of capacity, they would reorder. This lack of alignment was everywhere: reps only marginally cared about consumption, and many customers were oversold on bookings, which led to smaller renewals, or what we call down-sells, in future periods. The cost of commissions was out of whack with revenues because there was no direct relationship between sales compensation and revenues.

It took a few quarters to transition the company to consumption. Consumption became our middle name. We now looked at everything through the lens of consumption. We got better alignment.

Where alignment matters further is in incentive compensation. We pay everybody the same way on our executive team, and we have a very select, focused set of metrics that we pay bonuses on. Our sales exec does not get paid on a commission plan if the rest of us aren't. Everybody knows what we are aiming for.

Another source of misalignment is management by objectives (MBO), which I have eliminated at every company I've joined in the last 20 years. MBO causes employees to act as if they are running their own show. Because they get compensated on their personal metrics, it's next to impossible to pull them off projects. They will start negotiating with you for relief. That's not alignment, that's every man for himself. If you need MBO to get people to do their job, you may have the wrong people, the wrong managers, or both.

Sharpen Your Focus

Organizations are often spread too thinly across too many priorities, and too many of them are ill defined. Things tend to get added to the pile over time, and before we know it, we have huge backlogs. We're spread a mile wide and an inch deep. The problems with pace and tempo are, of course, related to having too much going on at the same time. It feels like swimming in glue, moving like molasses.

Leaders can do two things that bring almost instant benefit. First, think about execution more sequentially than in parallel. Work on fewer things at the same time, and prioritize hard. Even if you're not sure about ranking priorities, do it anyway. The process alone will be enlightening. Figure out what matters most, what matters less, and what matters not at all. Otherwise your people will disagree about what's important. The questions you should ask constantly: What are we *not* going to do? What are the consequences of *not* doing something? Get in the habit of constantly prioritizing and reprioritizing.

Most people have a relatively easy time coming up with their top three priorities. Just ask them. As an exercise I often ask: if you can only do one thing for the rest of the year, and nothing else, what would it be and why? People struggle with this question because it is easy to be wrong, which is exactly the point. If we are wrong, resources are misallocated. That's concerning. But we avoid these pointed dialogs because it is easier to list five or ten priorities. The right ones may not even be buried in there somewhere.

"Priority" should ideally only be used as a singular word. The moment you have many priorities, you actually have none.

At ServiceNow, I had such a "what is the one thing" conversation with our new chief product officer. Product organizations have a million things to do, and they really need to elevate their thinking to see the forest for the trees. This was not a quick or easy conversation, because it's easy to lose sight of the big picture when drowning in day-to-day obligations. I knew what I thought the answer should be, but would the CPO see it the same way? Did he even have a top priority?

What we arrived at was a singular focus on fashioning our rather industrial user experience to a consumer-grade service experience. This was not a short-term project; it would require a long-term shift in strategy, if not engineering culture, with sustained effort. It was important to the company's future yet also hard because it required changing our DNA. Our customers were IT people who had a high tolerance for these rather industrial, not very user-friendly experiences. The company had to forcibly move itself away from where it had come from. Having clarity is key, or people will just chip away at a problem, without significantly moving the needle. Intentions are often good, but they are then under-prioritized, under-resourced, and not fully crystalized.

Vagueness causes confusion, but clarity of thought and purpose is a huge advantage in business. Good leadership requires a never-ending process of boiling things down to their essentials. Spell out what you mean! If priorities are not clearly understood at the top, how distorted will they be down the line?

Pick Up the Pace

In a troubled organization there's no rush, no urgency. Why? People have to be there anyway, so what's the point in moving faster? If you have ever seen the inside of a California Department of Motor Vehicles (DMV), you know what that looks like. The staff doesn't start moving till 4:00 p.m. because quitting time is 4:30 p.m., and that backlog has to get cleared so everybody can depart on time. The rest of the day, who cares? They have to be there anyway.

Leaders set the pace. People sometimes ask to get back to me in a week, and I ask, why not tomorrow or the next day? Start compressing cycle times. We can move so much quicker if we just change the mindset. Once the cadence changes, everybody moves quicker, and new energy and urgency will be everywhere. Good performers crave a culture of energy.

It's not a one-time thing; it's not an email or a memo. It's using every encounter, meeting, and opportunity to increase the pace of whatever is going on. Apply pressure. Be impatient. Patience may be a virtue, but in business it can signal a lack of leadership. Nobody wants to swim in glue or struggle to get things done. Some organizations slow things down by design. Change that—ASAP.

Transform Your Strategy

Much of this book is about execution, especially developing relentless execution on your core mission. But that doesn't mean that strategy doesn't play an exceedingly important role. Once you know how to execute, you will become a better strategist, and strategy can become a force multiplier to your efforts. Transforming your strategy will require you to "widen the aperture" of your thinking about the business model, to reach new and bigger markets. You will need to develop peripheral vision, like a quarterback on a football field.

Thinking about strategy taxes a different part of our brains. It's more abstract, fluid, dynamic, multidimensional. It requires connecting seemingly unrelated things. This can drive the nuts-and-bolts type of people crazy. It's like strapping on a different mindset.

While everybody else has their head down, you need to have your head up, to confront both the need and the opportunity for strategic transformation. Develop a healthy sense of paranoia about your business model because your competitors are surely trying to disrupt you. That's as certain as the sun rising tomorrow.

The Epic Battle

After retiring from ServiceNow in 2017, I had no intention of ever taking another CEO position. But people like me—and I'm guessing people like you—have a hard time leaving the arena. It's exciting to be back in the fray as CEO of Snowflake, helping such a promising company deliver on its potential. It is an epic battle featuring new platforms, new competitors, new business models, all forward leaning and extremely stimulating. It is hard to back away from the constant rush of new experiences and learnings.

Leadership is a lonely business. You live 24/7 with uncertainty, anxiety, and the fear of personal failure. You make countless decisions, and being wrong about any of them might let down your employees and investors. The stakes, both financial and human, are high. And what adds to the terror is that there is no manual, no how-to guide. Every problem has, at least to some extent, never been seen before. In particular, early-stage enterprises often feel like they're shrouded in a fog of war.

My hope is that the chapters ahead will help you see through the fog, establish context, sort out your options, and amp up your organization on the road to success.

2

My Journey from Teenage Toilet Cleaner to Serial CEO

Before we continue, I should give you some background on how I developed and arrived at my "Amp It Up" approach to business. It has truly been a lifelong evolution across every job I've ever held. You'll hear more about my experiences in many of these roles in future chapters, but here is my overall journey.

A Childhood Grounded in Discipline

There is not much in my background that would foretell success as a Silicon Valley CEO. I grew up in a middle-class family in my native country of the Netherlands. I was the second of four siblings, half boys, half girls. We were never deprived of life's essentials, but there wasn't any money left over at the end of the month either.

My father was a veteran of two wars, and although he retired from active duty in the 1950s, there was a measure of discipline in our household. Walk straight, shoulders back, don't slouch. Proper meal etiquette: Nobody chowed down until everybody was properly seated, and somebody said, "*Eet Smakelijk*," the Dutch language equivalent of "Bon Appetit." Quick correction on improper use of silverware. Greet people with a firm handshake and look them in the eye. Never address elders by their first name. Don't let them catch you doing nothing, or they would find a chore for you to do. Play outside, never inside.

I had an episode in my early teens when my school grades were failing. My dad didn't say I needed to get better grades, merely that I had to work up to my potential. As long as I worked hard, he would accept the results. But he had to be fully convinced that I was in fact putting everything into it. That may appear to be a liberating way to have your parents think about failing grades. In reality, you become haunted by never doing enough, that you are failing to do as much as you are actually capable of.

In my teens, I held summer jobs that fueled my ambition. I harvested tulip bulbs at a farm in north Holland, walking the fields behind a tractor ten hours a day, in any weather. I also cleaned factory toilets one summer in the plant where my dad worked. There were at least a thousand people working there, and I cycled through every bathroom facility between 9:00 and 5:00. I had a supervisor, who inspected my work, but he often got to bathrooms I had cleaned first thing in the morning many hours later, after hundreds of people had used them. When he criticized my work, I complained about it to my dad. His answer was stark: "Well, those are the kinds of people you will be working for if you don't get better grades." I was 16.

This mentality of living up to your potential has kept up with me ever since. I am not so much focused day-to-day on outcomes; I am focused on maximizing the input side of the equation. Doing everything we can to the best of our abilities. It's like marathons or triathlons, which are 99% training and 1% racing. This is a hard model: you never feel you are doing enough, and a sense of malcontent hovers over you. You need like-minded people around you for this to work.

It also causes us to be not good at celebrations. We are so focused on the next thing that victory laps and self-congratulation are not in our DNA. They feel like we're jinxing ourselves. Instead, we always focus on the challenges in front of us.

Landing in the USA

I graduated cum laude from the Netherlands School of Economics, Erasmus University Rotterdam. I never failed a single exam, and I moved through the curriculum quickly. After three years I was a year ahead of schedule, so I took the time to do internships in the United States. I had never been to the US before.

I loved America. The people were welcoming and kind, and everybody always seemed to be in a positive, buoyant mood. It was such a contrast; where I came from people were more resigned to their fate, and whining was a national pastime. But Americans always seemed to think they could do better. The national spirit was quite energizing compared to what I was used to.

I returned to Holland a year later to finish school, write my doctoral thesis, and graduate. I was the only one in my family to graduate from university. Meanwhile, I was offered a follow-up internship, which led me back to the US. That's why I never really worked in my native land, and I didn't miss it. Perhaps I was born in the wrong country.

I landed in the US with about a hundred bucks in my pocket. I needed all sorts of help, which I readily received. Somebody handed me the keys to a 1974 Buick LeSabre and said, "Pay me when you can" and walked away. People were amazing. Since my internship at Uniroyal was temporary, I needed to land a real job and get my career going. Easier said than done. I spoke with a thick accent, fresh off the plane, with credentials that were hard to pronounce, let alone explain.

Uniroyal was a tire company that also made Naugahyde upholstery, a real smokestack industry. I was taken aback by what I saw there: layoffs, unions, evaporating markets. Back then, we thought the computer industry was the future. It wasn't a huge business yet, but at least it was dynamic and growing. I set my sights on IBM, the gold standard in computers in 1985. But I was rejected by IBM a dozen or so times before I gave up. They didn't know what to do with my European credentials. I have since realized that I was destined for a different path, and they were doing me a favor not hiring me.

Burroughs Corporation and Comshare

Burroughs Corporation was headquartered in Detroit, Michigan. They had a new CEO, Michael Blumenthal, a former Treasury secretary in the Carter administration and professor of economics from Princeton. My credentials perhaps looked less exotic there, and I got hired in a corporate planning role. Not what I wanted, but I figured I would make my way from there. We spent several years on what became Unisys, the merger of Burroughs and Sperry.

One major lesson stands out from those days. Burroughs thought that they were too small to compete with IBM, which was seen as a behemoth. So their strategy was to acquire scale by merging with Sperry. We have since learned that size isn't everything and often is a liability when things are changing rapidly. Every company I later ran would compete against much bigger companies, and our lack of size was an advantage. The big incumbents didn't know what hit them. Babies grow up to become soldiers.

We all need to be careful what "elevator" we get into early in our careers. Some go up, some go down, some don't move. It's largely beyond our control, so choose wisely. We have seen staggering examples of this phenomenon in Silicon Valley. Anybody who spent the last 20 years at Google, Amazon, or Apple would have done spectacularly well, regardless of their individual merit. And anyone who stayed with companies like IBM and HP would have stagnated during that period.

After five years at Burroughs/Unisys, I wanted to get into software, which was still a nascent industry in the 80s. Microsoft was established, but Oracle still seemed like a start-up. Unfortunately, geography was a factor. Michigan was a great place for automobiles but lousy for software. I landed a new job as a product manager for a time-sharing company in Ann Arbor called Comshare, which was developing "decision support systems," a forerunner of data analytics and online analytical processing.

At this point I was in my late twenties and desperate to get a shot at proving my mettle. I wanted to scream, "Give me any product, no matter how dreadful, and I will show you what I can do with it." It was not to be. Companies were more staid, hierarchical, and rigid then. They were not going to take a chance on this ornery upstart from Europe. Product management was a functional role that separated the ownership of various functions between different departments. I always operated as if I owned everything, whether I did or not. That didn't always sit well with peers or superiors. I have since always tried to increase our people's sense of ownership so they will act as owners. That mentality needs to be nurtured.

In an ill-advised move, fueled by frustration, I jumped to a start-up in Holland with some of my college pals. I knew almost immediately that it was a boneheaded move. In hindsight, I was feeling like a caged animal during this period. But in the long run it was helpful, because it broke the trajectory I was on.

Compuware

While still at Comshare, I had been getting recruiting calls from Compuware in Farmington Hills, Michigan. Compuware was growing and wanting to move into what we then called open systems—basically any platform other than IBM mainframes or DEC minicomputers. I was hired as the first non-mainframe open systems product manager at Compuware, which accelerated my career. Within seven years I would rise to VP and general manager, and I'd be well prepared for bigger challenges.

I only spent 18 months or so in their Michigan office. Compuware happened to acquire a Dutch company called UNIFACE, which developed cross-platform applications software. It wasn't long before they ran into trouble with the stubborn Dutch culture and needed a manager with a Dutch passport to help them sort through the issues. I jumped at the opportunity to return to Amsterdam and take on the entire operation, which seemed in disarray. Colleagues warned me not to go because the place could not be saved, and they thought I would go down with the ship. Compuware had bought UNIFACE toward the end of its viable product cycle.

But by now, my career had been about taking on what seemed like long odds, jobs nobody else would touch with a ten-foot pole. It was the only avenue open to me anyway, and it didn't matter to me how hairy these deals were. As a young person, you easily overestimate your capabilities. This is when I started learning what happens when you step into the wrong elevators.

We did manage to stabilize UNIFACE, and it is still around today, 25 years later. That became a formative career experience in my mid-30s. I had never had numerous large, mission critical customers before and hundreds of employees in my charge. I also started to develop an eye for talent, which became a cornerstone of my management focus going forward. I demanded plenty of myself but also of others. You can go far with good people, but they demand and deserve real leadership.

I was supposed to return to Michigan after three years, but Compuware had another fire burning, this time in California. The company had bought a series of start-ups in Silicon Valley and ran them as a single division, called EcoSystems. The set-in-their-ways Midwestern conservative values ran headlong into an ascending Silicon Valley. I arrived there in late 1997, the height of the tech bubble. Companies were going public on the strength of their eyeball metrics, not growth or profits.

We were caught between a rock and a hard place—the traditional, conservative business culture of the Midwest on the one hand and the radical, entrepreneurial ways of Silicon Valley on the other. We stabilized the struggling product lines we managed there, but we kept losing good talent because headquarters wouldn't let us match the salaries and equity offered by the dotcoms. Skilled workers flocked to other companies that were giving out promotions, pay raises, and share grants like Halloween candy. It was nuts. We had a sizable recruiting operation, but people left faster than they arrived.

We coped in ways I have used ever since: hire people ahead of their own curve. Hire more for aptitude than experience and give people the career opportunity of a lifetime. They will be motivated and driven, with a cannot-fail attitude. The good ones would grab the opportunity to accelerate their careers with us.

I still try to hire more for aptitude than experience. We don't always require been-there, done-that types. Checking boxes on a resume is easy. Assessing aptitude is harder. Look for hunger, attitude, innate abilities. Perhaps, look for the same career-frustrated person I had been all these years. It was quite satisfying to turn this into a high-powered strategy to drive business. I ended up with better, cheaper, more loyal, more motivated talent than we would have with a conventional hiring mentality. It does come with risk, but there is always risk in hiring. I have misfired with great resumes plenty of times.

Borland

Mid-year 2000 I cut the Compuware cord and joined Borland as SVP of product operations, basically running everything except sales and corporate functions. Borland was another former name-brand highflier with a loyal, if not fanatical, developer following. But it had fallen on hard times, even changing its name to Inprise. We changed the name back and resurrected the Borland brand and business. Borland did well on the Sun Microsystems Java platform with its line of software developer tools. Now pushing 40, I was still taking on problem children.

Having left the Midwestern womb of Compuware, I started to become more networked in Silicon Valley. You can go to an infinite number of meetings in Silicon Valley. Recruiters, venture capital firms, and any number of companies that want to buy, sell, invest, or hire. The place sometimes feels like a single beehive that is reconstituting new companies all the time.

I quickly learned that my seven years at Compuware, and all the things I had done there, impressed few people in the Valley. I did start getting calls for CEO roles of start-ups in trouble, basically the bottom of the venture pile. I was cautioned along the way by industry friends to hold out as long as it took. Avoid the second- and third-string deals, which would probably be elevators to nowhere.

I got rejected for better deals over and over with the same excuse: you have never run sales. While that was true, I was (in my own estimation) a highly sales-oriented product person. How would I ever check that box? You don't just cross over into sales after having been a product person all your career. I led from the front and sold shoulder-to-shoulder with sales. These rejections left me with an unfavorable opinion of many venture capitalists who could not recognize talent if it smacked them in the face.

I would later get some satisfaction over the naysayers by serving as CEO of three of the fastest-growing companies in Silicon Valley history.

Data Domain

Finally, in the spring of 2003, I got tapped for an early-stage start-up called Data Domain. It had no revenues, no customers. What piqued my interest was the investors: Aneel Bhusri of Greylock and Scott Sandell of NEA—accomplished VCs from top-tier firms. They saw through my unconventional credentials and that I would simply refuse to fail. Data Domain had a founder, Dr. Kai Lee, a computer science professor who had to go back to Princeton in the fall, and they needed a CEO. I became the first (and only) CEO of Data Domain in July 2003.

At that point Silicon Valley was a wasteland following the bursting of the dotcom bubble. The talent game was easier because of sagging demand, but raising venture capital was harder. Things felt slow and lethargic. Start-ups were seen as risky by employees. Customers wanted to buy their data storage from large, low-risk providers such as EMC and NetApp. The whole Valley felt like it had a giant hangover. So Data Domain was far from a sure thing. There was no way to know. We were one of hundreds of start-ups in the enterprise technology space.

We also got lectured by our VCs on other companies that supposedly were role models for us. Some of these companies you could not even recall today. I still apologize to CEOs who in later years were lectured on Data Domain as a role model. One of the more irritating habits VCs have is "pattern matching," making recommendations and suggestions based on what other supposedly successful companies were doing. No two companies are alike, and just because another company is doing it, doesn't make it right.

Our initial experiences at Data Domain were not inspiring. We had a backup disk storage array that had a well-designed data de-duplication capability built in. It filtered out redundant segments on the fly, or inline, as we used to say. And it did so with speed and at low cost. Our architecture was superior and became an enduring differentiator. We still say, "Architecture matters" at Snowflake; all of our successes at the three companies where I've been CEO trace back to superior architecture.

But our inaugural DD200 backup storage array was small, slow, and had few viable use cases to keep a sales function alive. We could not back up anything at scale like a file system or a database. We debated going back into R&D mode until we had a larger, faster product. But we were rightly afraid we could not raise money on that basis. Venture capital equaled oxygen in those days. You managed a start-up from one fundraising milestone to another back then.

We sold what we could with a "two men and a dog" effort that first year and racked up $3 million in sales. The product doubled in size and speed, and the next year we ramped up sales to $15 million. "Larger *and* faster" became our mantra, like those old commercials for Miller Lite Beer, "Less Filling—Tastes Great." We never backed off that.

Now that we had figured out the formula, we scaled the hell out of the business as fast as the technology roadmap would allow. From $15 million, we went to $45 million, to $125 million, and then to $275 million in annual revenues. I still remember one board meeting when the directors slowly realized we had doubled the size of the entire company inside a quarter. As a hardware platform, Data Domain had product margins in the low 80s, like a software product.

Data Domain went public on Nasdaq in 2007, after an almost six-year IPO drought on Wall Street. In 2009, it was acquired by EMC after a high-profile, public bidding war with NetApp. EMC is today part of Dell, and I am told reliably that Data Domain is still, more than ten years later, a top profit contributor in that product portfolio. EMC massively accelerated Data Domain's distribution, and it rapidly became a multibillion-dollar business, which it still is today. Joe Tucci, EMC's CEO, remarked that after VMWare, Data Domain was the best deal he ever did. It was also the biggest acquisition EMC ever did.

Data Domain consumed net venture capital of $28 million from inception, and six years later returned $2.4 billion to shareholders—the magic of combining capital with talent, the essence of economics and capitalism. As a former economics academic, I now had a better appreciation of what I had been studying years ago in Rotterdam.

Transitions: EMC and Greylock

I went along with the deal to EMC, as EVP and division president. Not because I really wanted to work for EMC but because I felt honor-bound after selling a multibillion-dollar asset to protect both the business and the people. That turned out to be necessary. EMC's CEO wisely asked us to take on all of EMC's data protection products. He had good reason: they were mostly languishing or in decline. Products easily get neglected in larger companies. Underperforming tech assets seemed to follow me around like a bad habit.

We had sold the company to EMC in large part because they had the complementary storage assets that Data Domain didn't. All we had to do was fix and integrate these products, and the legendary EMC sales and channel organization would do the rest. That's what happened. The division became a formidable grower and profit contributor in short order. Then, as previously agreed with EMC, I left after 18 months.

After working with venture capitalists for years, I decided to try my hand at that aspect of the tech world. So I joined the VC firm Greylock as a partner. Many people openly speculated I would not last, and they were right. I was not only not ready; I also lacked the temperament for a venture partnership. Greylock is a fine firm, but we simply weren't a good match. Most venture firms are partnerships, without a chain of command. They are highly collegial—everybody is expected to get along and make decisions together. I felt like a fish out of water.

ServiceNow

In 2011 I started discussions with the fast-growing ServiceNow.com, a San Diego–based company that had that relaxed Southern California lifestyle flavor all over it. Work seemed down the list of priorities there. ServiceNow was already at a $75 million revenue run rate; the infamous start-up "chasm," as popularized by management author Geoffrey Moore, had scarcely been a speed bump. Amazingly, the company had been bootstrapped with only $6–7 million in capital, and it had managed to put $50 million in cash on the balance sheet from operations.

The company was still being run by its founder and CEO but was unduly controlled by its finance function: it was literally starving for resources. When I met the R&D department, it turned out that was just the founder and a handful of his cronies. On the P&L, R&D did not even break 2% of revenues. You would normally expect that percentage to be 15–20 times larger in a company at this stage of evolution. As the new CEO, I set out to change that ASAP.

Our so-called cloud was a hosting service. The company had large early adopters including GE, Johnson & Johnson, and Deutsche Bank, and I would receive frantic calls from their CIOs wondering what was going on. I shared their anxiety. I was anxious to pick up the phone or open my email in the morning for a good year and a half. There was not only a lot of work to do; we didn't really know how to do it. There was nobody in the company who had ever built a cloud computing platform before.

Meanwhile, we kept acquiring and onboarding customers. We were not a real cloud in the computer science meaning of the word. We were a hosted service, meaning that each customer had their own hardware and software instances. ServiceNow was not what was called "multi-tenant," where customers share computing resources. We ended up hooking up with some early eBay pioneers who had real experience, which in hindsight was also limited, but it was a damn sight more than what we knew back then.

Not many people on the outside, or even on the inside, knew how close ServiceNow came to blowing itself up. One Friday, a free-lancing technician inadvertently upgraded 800 customers, breaking or disrupting all their systems. We still refer to this day as Black Friday; I still don't know how we managed to live through it. After that, freelancing became a "one strike and you're out" offense.

Some of our executives were pleading with me to sell the company because they were scared and overwhelmed. Fred Luddy, our founder, once said we were like a truck rambling down the side of a mountain with one lug nut partially tightened on each wheel. It felt like we would blow apart at any moment.

Founder Fred Luddy and I butted heads in the early going. He even remarked that he regretted bringing me and my colleagues on to run the company. On one email thread, he announced he was going to override me. I had to explain that there is no such thing as an override for CEOs. I said, "You can go to the board and see if they'd like to fire me and give you your old job back. In the mean-time, we are doing as I outlined." Fred came around eventually and ended up being a fan, but it took a while. Change can be hard.

ServiceNow pulled it together painstakingly over the course of two anxious years. We never slowed the company down; on the contrary we kept pouring fuel on the fire. We were not going to squander this opportunity, no matter what. We were growing at a blistering pace and trying to build the service at the same time. Our culture became much more grounded, methodical, and analytical in staring down its challenges. One foot in front of the other. One brick in the wall after another. We hired but also fired a lot of people in those early days of rapid growth.

What haunted me from the Data Domain experience was the pressing need for transformation that we had failed to execute on. That was why we ended up selling. At Data Domain, we had been landlocked and would run out of market, with no potential avenues of expansion beyond our core backup and recovery business, short of making massive acquisitions. We did not have the balance sheet or the market cap to grow via acquisitions. EMC did, and the rest is history.

Now I was focused on how ServiceNow could expand beyond its initial total addressable market (TAM) to avoid Data Domain's fate. Once burned, twice shy. As I went through the CEO interview process with the board of directors, I kept hearing about customers who used the product in completely different domains than IT. The ServiceNow people actually didn't think much of that, but it registered as a big deal to me. It looked like this was a generic service management workflow platform that could be adapted for any service domain. The market was signaling that.

Once we got beyond our urgent, short-term operational challenges, we expanded the company from licensing just the help desk management staff to everybody in the IT function, a much larger universe of employees. The idea was that everybody in the IT department was involved in the workflow to resolve incidents. Not just the help desk but also system and database administrators, network engineers, and application developers. ServiceNow became a system of record as well as a system of engagement for the entire IT department. It was becoming the chief information officer's system.

The expanded positioning enabled us to move higher in the customer's organization, do bigger deals, and truly become a strategic IT management platform for large enterprises.

Once that was underway, we expanded even more by launching a half dozen business units in service domains outside of enterprise IT. They used the underlying ServiceNow software platform but adapted it for new uses at the application level. We now had unique products for each service area. I expected only a few of these service lines to make it, but they all caught fire, some more than others. Our new organizational model enabled the teams to excel under their own power without excessive dependency on outside organizations. ServiceNow became an ideal training ground for executives with raw drive, something to prove, and a chip on their shoulder. I enjoyed helping them develop as leaders.

We even ventured into service cloud territory, using Service-Now for customer support. We had some strong advocates internally for this because we used it ourselves that way. I held them off, not believing we could go that far afield that soon. It was a very different buying center than what we were used to; we didn't even know these people, and they didn't know us. The product demands in this service area were also more consumer oriented than enterprise oriented, a higher standard of user interface sophistication. I relented, still not convinced, but it turned out I was wrong. This new source of revenue did work—in fact, it took off. There are times you need to check your own views at the door and bet on the conviction of others.

Our positioning further expanded to the point that large enterprises designated ServiceNow as their workflow platform for all service domains. Employees interacted with just one system, ServiceNow, and no longer needed to navigate their organizations to find functions and people who could address their incidents, issues, questions, and tasks. Some large companies created new teams to run what they called global business services on ServiceNow. ServiceNow had evolved to a service workflow platform without limits. I sometimes referred to it as a "structured messaging platform" in contrast to the unstructured messaging of email, text, and numerous other messaging services. Structured meant the data was defined inside the message or task, and logic could operate without limit on it.

When we announced plans to take the company public on the New York Stock Exchange in 2012, there were plenty of naysayers who did not believe in us. Gartner Group hosted so-called fireside chats with investors during our roadshow, basically questioning everything we were messaging. The detractors eventually had to admit that they were flat-out wrong about ServiceNow. As I write this, its market capitalization is above $100 billion and still growing.

A Very Brief Retirement

I didn't know it at the time, but by 2017 I was burnt out. After too many years in the line of fire, I felt like I didn't have much left to give. So I stepped down and handed the reins to John Donahoe, former CEO of eBay. ServiceNow was in formidable shape, and I believed that our previous three years had put us on a growth trajectory that would be next to impossible to derail. Bill McDermott, former CEO of SAP, took over from Donahoe in 2019, and the company continues on a tear to this day.

The first few weeks of my retirement, in April 2017, were liberating, even euphoric. Not going to work on Monday and not feeling the quarterly gun on my forehead felt awesome. After decades of hard work, I finally had plenty of free time.

I spent a lot more time on my passion for regatta sailing. My team raced a TP52 named *Invisible Hand* in California, Mexico, and Hawaii regattas. The highlight of those racing seasons was winning the 2017 Transpac, an iconic ocean race, which has been sailed every other year since 1906. It starts in Los Angeles and goes all the way to Oahu, Hawaii. Just as in business, we focused on recruiting great talent. The *Invisible Hand* had a crackerjack team of professional sailors, and I was thrilled to be on the ocean with them.

Aside from sailing, I joined some of my VC friends in investing in early-stage companies, and I served on a few boards. I admit that I am not the best board member: I get impatient and struggle with the hands-off relationship boards are supposed to have with management. As I had learned at Greylock, I have the temperament of an operator, not an investor/advisor.

One of the boards I was serving on was Pure Storage, a successful flash storage array company that had been bootstrapped before its IPO by Mike Speiser of Sutter Hill Ventures. Mike is a one-of-a-kind VC: he comes up with brand-new ideas, recruits extremely high-end talent, and launches them as a start-up, often acting as the company's first CEO.

Along with Pure, Mike had also bootstrapped Snowflake in 2012. We would sometimes get together to compare notes, including updates on Snowflake's progress. Mike wanted me to join Snowflake's board, but nothing ever came of it. This was when I was focused on sailboat racing. Then one March afternoon in 2019, Mike and I had lunch, and he blurted out, "What would it take for you to take the helm at Snowflake?" My reaction: "What?"

I hadn't decided to take the field again at all. I had not even considered it as a serious possibility. Whenever someone asked, my pat answer was always "never say never." I never talked to another company. But Snowflake was special—it had built a data management platform for the new cloud scale computing platforms of

Amazon Web Services (AWS), Microsoft Azure, and Google Cloud Platform (GCP). Snowflake founders were hard-core technologists, steeped in state-of-the-art database technology. They didn't want to carry that legacy forward to the cloud. Instead, they reimagined and reinvented data management top to bottom. It was virtually a clean sheet of paper exercise, which rarely happens in tech.

It is unlikely that a company other than Snowflake would have persuaded me to get back in the arena, but the opportunity to become its CEO was hard to resist. Today I am less driven by career ambition than by a hunger for sport, action, excitement, teamwork, and a never-ending pursuit of self-improvement. Being retired was great, but the challenge of rising to the occasion is a better match for my temperament.

Snowflake

I hit the ground running on April 26, 2019. On the upside, Snowflake was already on a tear, and its recent results were mesmerizing. Core data management processes such as complex queries and data ingestion ran one or two orders of magnitude faster than they had previously in on-premise data centers. It had innovated on multiple vectors at once: it addressed much larger data volumes, dramatically increased computational performance, and enabled virtually unlimited concurrent execution of workloads. You could fire up as many workloads as you had appetite and budget for. You could run them as often as you pleased and had budget for. You could over-provision workloads and make them run much, much faster than ever before. And it used a utility model: you could commandeer as much resource as you wanted, for as long as you wanted, and just get charged for what you actually consumed.

On the downside, the company was quite impressed with itself, precisely because growth was off the charts. I began to understand why Mike was so anxious about the leadership and had convinced the board to consider a leadership change. Snowflake had an amazing product, but its execution was increasingly questionable. The P&L revealed that this was a company with a lot of funding but not much discipline. Without any dramatic changes, it might still have a great exit at, say, $10 billion in value. But why not go for $100 billion or more? The opportunity was right there if we could just amp things up.

The first few weeks of my tenure were messy, as I quickly removed many of the department heads from their positions. The previous CEO had more than a dozen direct reports, but I was planning on only five or six. Change was coming fast, and I caught flak for removing folks I didn't know well. Critics said I should have given everyone a fair chance to prove that they could meet my expectations, but I didn't see it that way. I wanted to eliminate uncertainty and doubt by bringing in some sure-fire executives that I had worked with at previous companies. When you take over a company with a wide range of issues, you have to start solving the more straightforward problems as fast as possible so you can narrow the focus on the harder ones. Bringing in some proven performers was a no-brainer.

For instance, I had first hired Mike Scarpelli as CFO of Data Domain in 2006, and when I joined ServiceNow in 2011, I got the board to approve him for the same role before I even started. Now I approached Mike again, even before I decided to take the CEO job at Snowflake. We were a package deal; I probably would have declined if Mike had not agreed to be my copilot again. I play offense while Mike plays defense, making him a perfect counterpart for me. We tend to have short conversations because we're aligned on standards and priorities. The Snowflake board gave Mike a contract as CFO.

To be sure, Snowflake already had a lot of truly outstanding people, especially on the product and marketing sides. There were issues in sales, but I took more time picking my way through that essential part of the business. It's like surgery; if you're indiscriminate, you may hurt more than help, and we couldn't afford to cripple our sales momentum. The corporate functions, on the other hand, were barely breathing and needed many changes.

The product operation had several different leaders trying to drive conflicting priorities. We removed some and then elevated our co-founder Benoit Dageville to president of products, consolidating the product leadership. We hired a new top-flight executive in Greg Czajkowski to run engineering, and that team is functioning better now than ever before; that is according to our Snowflake veterans.

We went public on the NYSE on September 16, 2020, about a year and half after our team arrived. It was billed as the biggest software IPO in history, and one of the biggest tech IPOs ever, with our stock massively bidding up to a $70+ billion market valuation. Everybody wanted a part of Snowflake.

Becoming an Amped-Up Leader

The biggest difference between younger me and older me is that I am now much quicker to grasp what's really going on and what needs to happen to amp up an organization. Years ago, I used to hesitate and wait situations out, often trying to fix underperforming people or products instead of pulling the plug. Back then I was seen as a much more reasonable and thoughtful leader—but that didn't mean I was right. As I got more experience, I realized that I was often just wasting everybody's time. If we knew that something or someone wasn't working, why wait? As the saying goes, when there is doubt, there is no doubt.

The rest of this book will give you a deeper understanding of how to do the same at your own organization. You too can become great at quickly figuring out what to keep, what to jettison, and what to fix on the journey to a mission-driven, high-performance company.

PART

II

Raise Your Standards

3

Make Your Organization Mission Driven

What Does It Mean to Be Mission Driven?

The term that best describes the management mindset of all three companies I've led (Data Domain, ServiceNow, and Snowflake) is *mission driven*. A clear and compelling sense of mission has been one of the essential keys to our consistent success and growth. Time after time, our focused missions helped us relentlessly pursue each company's promise and potential. Being mission driven helped our people become motivated, focused, impatient, and passionate—maybe even a bit zealous.

Being on a mission is a *visceral* experience, not merely an intellectual one. When your organization has a well-defined purpose, you feel it down to your bones. You feel energized when you start the workday, and you feel good about whatever progress you've made toward the mission when you shut down for the night. Being on a mission unlocks the X factor: an intangible that can drastically elevate performance as people set out to achieve greatness—together. It makes your working life not just more productive but also more fun.

Conversely, you're not on a mission if you feel like you spend most of your days checking off trivial to-do items, passing the buck to other people, reading and forwarding email, and covering your ass so you won't get in any trouble. Showing up every day at a "good enough is good enough" company is the opposite of fun and energizing. Just trying to get through each day is a depressing way to spend a career. And if most people at your company feel that way, the enterprise is in grave danger.

I didn't invent the term *mission driven*, of course. In my naivete, I used to think that the importance of having a mission was self-evident. Of course every company should know exactly why it exists and what it's trying to accomplish, and of course it should communicate that purpose clearly to everyone. Who would even think to argue the opposite? Perhaps a clear purpose was common a few decades ago, but these days I see more and more companies that are fuzzy, if not hopelessly confused, about why they exist. The mission clarity that used to be the norm has now become more of an exception—which gives leaders who get it right a competitive advantage.

Now let's look at the three criteria for a great mission: big, clear, and not about money.

A Great Mission Is Big (but Not Impossible!)

Snowflake's current mission is to mobilize the world's data by building the world's greatest data and applications platform, not just of the cloud era, but in the history of computing. This is a wildly ambitious vision! It massively exceeds in scale and scope what any company has tried to do in this space. We will not simply coast toward that goal, because the world will not let us. But the more determined and focused we are as a group, the greater the odds that we can reach this status. It's hardly impossible.

At Data Domain, our mission was to put tape automation out of existence as a data backup and recovery platform and replace it with ultra-efficient, high-speed disks and networks. Our mantra was "Tape sucks"—we were taking on the entire industry's status quo. That was another wildly ambitious vision, and we ultimately achieved it. Backup and recovery became a fully digital, automated process across the industry, which helped everyone, except for the tape automation companies that didn't move with the times.

ServiceNow set out to become the new global standard for IT service and operations management. We saw that the prior generation of help desk management products were almost universally loathed by IT people. They were rigid and technically cumbersome. IT staffs would rarely upgrade their systems because it was so time-consuming, expensive, risky, and of marginal benefit. We set a huge goal of making life better for every IT person in the country, if not the world. Today it sometimes seems like absolutely everybody in that space is using ServiceNow.

A Great Mission Is Clear

The more defined and intense the mission, the easier it will be for everyone to focus on it. When issues and topics unrelated to the mission come up, people will naturally give them less mindshare than they otherwise might. A great mission helps prevent distractions that dilute everyone's focus. In every company I've ever encountered, distractions are a huge threat. They often become a major source of self-defeating behavior.

Continually narrowing the mission aperture is key because companies have a natural tendency to lose focus over time. It's incredibly easy for managers to react to every headline that crosses their email inbox, Slack, or social media feeds. If you turn your time and attention to the latest shiny object, regardless of how little it has to do with your mission, you are on the path to trouble. Distractions will inevitably pop up every day and need to be fought relentlessly.

Military history shows us the power of a well-defined mission. During World War II, the US had an extremely clear mission: stop the fascist dictators from taking over the world. Likewise, when the Navy's Seal Team Six was dispatched to Pakistan to take out terrorist mastermind Osama Bin Laden, deep in hostile territory, the daring mission it had and a crystal-clear purpose drove a detailed, well-rehearsed plan, informed by intelligence on the ground. It succeeded without any loss of life on our side.

But defining a mission clearly is more easily said than done. In the decades since World War II, the US has gotten caught up in several ambiguous wars with ill-conceived definitions of success—notably Vietnam but also Iraq and Afghanistan. It's hard to forget former president George W. Bush declaring, "Mission accomplished" on the flight deck of the aircraft carrier USS Abraham Lincoln on May 1, 2003, after the initial victorious phase of the Iraq war. Tragically, that war was really just starting because deposing Saddam Hussein left the unresolved question of who would now be in charge in Iraq and who would prevent its internal factions from fighting each other. Hundreds of thousands of lives and trillions of dollars were arguably wasted because we invaded Iraq without a clear, well-planned mission.

For a more recent example, remember that when the Coronavirus pandemic first hit the US, lockdowns were described as a short-term strategy to stop the contagion from overwhelming our healthcare system. But before long, lockdowns became the designated method to control the pandemic indefinitely, dragging on in many states for well over a year. Pandemic responses began to seem like a "make it up as we go along" approach to policy, completely untethered from any clear mission.

People use the term *mission creep* when an organization's stated purpose keeps changing and/or being redefined. We must show constant vigilance against the risk of mission creep.

A Great Mission Is Not About Money

It's essential to make it clear to everyone that your organization's purpose is *not* exceeding Wall Street's quarterly expectations or other financial targets. Those are milestones along the way to your true mission. Not that there's anything wrong with financial metrics or showing progress to investors or shareholders. I take those targets very seriously, but they are never our mission. All of our companies had a true purpose of bringing good things to the world and improving the lives of our customers and employees. Our innovative products changed the status quo.

Data Domain changed the IT industry's dependency on tape automation, the standard for system backup and recovery since the beginning of computing. Our disk- and network-based platform was faster, dead-certain of a successful recovery, and economically superior. The jobs and roles associated with tape backup were miserable, so there was no love lost for the old technology. People would often spend all night or all weekend babysitting these backups and recoveries. Tape backups are brittle, they often fail, and all it takes for disaster is one bad tape in the sequence. We often joked that tape backup was pretty good, as long as you never needed to recover data from it.

At ServiceNow, our mission was to become the "enterprise resource planning for IT" and later to be a global business services workflow platform for all service domains. ServiceNow became an immensely popular product with IT staffs because it was so approachable by mere mortals and so easily modified as the need arose. We won because IT people adopted it as "their" system.

Snowflake set out to reinvent the fundamentals of big-data processing, which previously took place on specialized data ware-housing platforms as well as large-scale general database manage-ment platforms from the likes of Oracle and Microsoft. Workloads often ran orders of magnitude faster with Snowflake technology, a mind-blowing experience for many of our customers. People finally saw the real power of cloud computing in action. We developed an instant following as a game-changer, which continues to this day. Our Data Cloud, an ambitious, never-done-before cloud data plat-form, is transforming entire industries and careers.

Between the three companies, we've created hundreds of billions of dollars of market value. As previously observed, Data Domain consumed net capital of $28 million and was acquired by EMC for $2.4 billion years later in 2009. ServiceNow was bootstrapped with $6.5 million of capital and is now valued well north of $100 billion. Snowflake had over $5 billion on its balance sheet post-IPO and now has a market capitalization in excess of $75 billion.

Critics may say that most of this value creation goes to investors and executives, but that's not the whole story. Investors and execu-tives take huge risks on start-ups that need to be rewarded when a company is successful. But most of our staff also participate mean-ingfully in value creation. Even modest equity allocations can lead to life-changing gains for employees, which they can apply to buy-ing homes, educating their children, taking care of their loved ones, and securing their retirements. This realization was never far from my mind: Our people were counting on me because the company's fate could have a profound effect on their futures.

I would sometimes say in all-hands meetings that I was personally committed to help each of our employees reach a different station in life as a function of the company's fortunes. In exchange, I was asking for the best they had to offer. That was the deal: we do the best we can for each other. People sometimes gave me an incredulous look: a CEO who is saying that his goal is to elevate our fortunes? Seriously? Yes, and our companies proved it. Sometimes years after a staffer had moved on, I would still receive an email expressing their appreciation for how much our company had changed their life's trajectory.

How to Nurture the Mission

Once you have your mission in place, how do you get everyone to embrace it and make it real? The four keys are applying focus, urgency, execution, and strategy.

If people don't *focus* on the mission, they are not really on a mission. We concentrate our resources and bandwidth on the mission, and we avoid distractions. That takes discipline. Distractions that can jeopardize the mission are everywhere, and they often seem well-intentioned, honorable, and worthwhile. For instance, companies are now expected to cater to any number of so-called stakeholders, while addressing societal ills such as climate change and social injustice. But once you get knocked off your mooring by external goals, it's hard to get back to the main mission that you're supposed to be focusing on.

The mission also has to be treated with *urgency*. There is a saying in sales that "time kills all deals." Time is not our friend. Time introduces risks, such as new entrants. The faster we separate from the competition, the more likely we are to succeed. Urgency is a mindset that can be learned if it doesn't come to you naturally.

You can embrace the discomfort that comes with moving faster instead of avoiding it. More pep in our step energizes the workplace culture, making everything seem lighter, quicker, and easier. When everyone on the team embraces urgency, we all move at a similar pace, without being slowed down by distractions.

We have to *execute* on our mission via an organized, orchestrated, and resourced set of activities. We have no chance accomplishing it without a drive for world-class execution, which includes high standards and efficient use of resources. For instance, a few months after D-Day, the British had attempted to win World War II by launching the largest airborne operation in history, to take the City of Arnhem in Holland and four bridges over major rivers leading up to it. It failed due to poor execution, with even more loss of life than the Normandy invasion the previous June. Intelligence failures were to blame, but the mission was also put together in less than 10 days—far too brief for a mission this risky and at this enormous scale.

Finally, the mission has to be kept in mind when we devise the *strategy* that we execute on. Strategies don't change day-to-day, only when there is a demonstrably better way to do things or if something just isn't working, unrelated to execution failure. Everyone needs to feel confident that our strategy is in line with the goals of our mission. Going back to World War II, one reason the Normandy invasion worked was that the strategy was brilliant: simultaneous attacks over the water and from the air, opening up five different beachheads, only one of which was heavily defended by the Germans. The enemy was caught by surprise, which gave the Allies a fighting chance to execute on their strategy and fulfill their mission.

Living the Mission Every Day

As I go through my week, I continually filter whatever comes over the transom through the lens of Snowflake's mission. Will this help us get to the data cloud faster? What else can we do to move closer to the mission and get there quicker? Until the mission is fulfilled, I will never be fully satisfied with the status quo.

It's not easy to live with the constant angst that we might not be doing enough. It would be more fun to do victory laps and pat everybody on the back all the time. But in the end, we will be all be better off because of our intensely vigilant posture toward our mission. We won't rest on our laurels. The competition is getting more aggressive by the day, so this is no time to relax our focus.

Many companies claim to be mission driven because it sounds high-minded. But as with other management clichés, such as "performance culture" and "customer centric," talking the talk is much easier than walking the walk. Don't listen to what leaders say—watch what they do. Mission driven is not just what you believe, it's how you make decisions every day about your time and effort and resources. It's about delivering on your most important promises, not racking up style points. It's about making choices during every meeting and every interaction. Grinding away toward your mission, day in and day out, will absolutely pay off.

Snowflake hired some 800 new teammates in 2020, and we continue to grow rapidly. New folks can't help but bring some of their old culture from whence they came. Many companies out there are not like us and have a much more casual approach to their mission. But as far as Snowflake is concerned, this is nonnegotiable: we expect everybody to embrace the Snowflake mission with everything they've got. This company is counting on our people 100%. All hands on deck, at all times.

4

Declare War on Your Competitors and on Incrementalism

The War Against Your Competitors

It's no exaggeration to say that business is war. Either you already have a turf, and you have to defend it against all comers, or else you have to invade somebody else's turf and take it. We are playing defense and offense at the same time. Either way, conflict is inevitable. Only the government can print money; the rest of us have to take it from somebody else. I love a win-win deal as much as anyone else, but it's much more common that business is close to a zero-sum game.

Part of your responsibility as a leader is making this crystal clear to your people. In today's polite society, many of them will resist the metaphor of war. Life is plenty ugly already; can't we be more civilized about competing with other firms? You'll have to teach them that the game doesn't really start until the other guys, whose profits you are trying to seize, start fighting back with everything they have. They are not our friendly competitors. At a minimum, noses will get bloodied. At worst, in a few months or years, some firms in our industry will still be in business and others won't.

Not everyone has this visceral sense of contest, especially at companies that shield their people from the real stakes at hand. When leaders fail to explain the industry landscape, employees don't feel the cold winds of competition. Their jobs and paychecks feel secure, but that's an illusion. Good leaders explain that none of us are ever truly safe in our roles for any length of time. If this fact makes people uncomfortable, that's good. You need to get comfortable with being uncomfortable because the only alternative is denialism.

At Data Domain, competing against EMC meant competing against free, which is always extremely hard. What we charged for, because we only had one product, they included for free with their other products and services. In the tech world, we refer to this practice as "bundling." We got in the habit of saying that "free isn't free" because products have to be operated and managed, which of course costs money. We used to say to potential customers, "What's the real cost of something free that doesn't do the job properly? How would you like a free elephant, if you have to feed, house, and clean up after it?"

At ServiceNow, our arch-competitor BMC sued us for intellectual property infringement. They could not compete on product, so they found other ways of inflicting damage. We ended up settling for hundreds of millions of dollars. We viewed the suit as bogus, but truth didn't matter; the question was what a slick lawyer might get a jury to believe. The legal system will always be exploited by those who cannot compete on merit. The legality of a business tactic doesn't matter; it's all about what people can get away with.

At Snowflake, it is common for the public cloud vendors to buy out technical debt, meaning that they find ways to make past financial obligations go away, heavily subsidize expensive software migrations for free, and provide all matter of free and bundled stuff. Like refinancing your mortgage, only more lucrative. They don't want to compete on product because that levels the playing field, which would yield a highly uncertain outcome. Instead, they use their formidable scale to squash competition. As a smaller company, we have to fight back with the superiority of our product and the sponsors inside accounts—people who really want our product and do the internal selling on our behalf. We see very large institutions choose Snowflake because the preference of grassroots IT managers was so strong, even though the politics at the corporate level were massively against us. The politics were rooted in past relationships but also in what's called the balance of trade. If a vendor is also a big buyer of the customer's products and services, they will use that to tip the scales. Very few things are off limits in the battle for the customer. Executives are afraid though to ram a vendor down the throats of their employees because they may just move on to a company that lets them work with their preferred products.

We even see this competition approach in existing Snowflake accounts, buy out everything under contract with us, fund the migration, and provide all matter of bundles and free computing credits that can be applied to workload execution. (Antitrust enforcers get upset if you overcharge customers, but they are fine with giving things away, even if your intent is to put your competition out of business.) It's not just about winning business, it's also about inflicting maximum public embarrassment on us. If they ever take one of our key accounts that way, they will parade it around the entire industry. Like it or not, that's also a part of warfare against your competitors.

In sales meetings I would sometimes pose a clarifying question: "What is our definition of victory? Sun Tzu, in *The Art of War*, had a simple answer: 'Breaking the enemy's will to fight.'" That translates in business terms to persuading some of your competition's best talent to join your company instead. The more high-achieving people who desert their current employers to join us, the more we are winning. It's a double whammy: not only is our enemy losing some of its best talent, but we've taken their strength. A talent drain is the best evidence that a company is in serious trouble and is losing its will to fight.

The War Against Incrementalism

Another human tendency is to approach things incrementally, from an abundance of caution. It feels safer to inch forward rather than take bold leaps. Incrementalism is about avoiding risk by building on whatever has already been achieved as a stable foundation. But merely trying for marginal improvements on the status quo carries its own risks.

Note how often consumer goods products are marketed as "new and improved." That's incrementalism, basically telling customers it's the same product they already know and love but even better. In other words, don't worry, we didn't take anything away from you. People prefer the familiarity of the known over the uncertainty of the unknown. That's a fine strategy for long-established brands in categories such as breakfast cereal or toothpaste. It's also fine for industries such as aviation, where change has to come very slowly because there are so many regulatory hurdles to dramatic change.

But in most fields, incrementalism is merely a lack of audacity and boldness. Maybe you won't lose, but you won't win either.

Larger, established enterprises are especially prone to incremental behavior because risks are not rewarded—but screwups are severely punished. Many of these companies end up killing themselves gradually, through stagnation. That's why very few enterprises that were in the Fortune 500 just 50 years ago still exist. A living organism like a business needs to reinvent itself all the time, rather than just consolidate and extend past gains.

Rather than seeking incremental progress from the current state, try thinking about the future state you want to reach and then work backward to the present. What needs to happen to get there? This exercise can be inspiring and motivating, as you become guided by your future vision. Don't try to steer the ship by looking at its wake!

I've seen how incrementalism can suck the life force out of people and organizations. In too many internal meetings, managers articulate their goals in terms of the delta from where they are today. "We want to have 30% more customers in two years." That sounds safe and respectable, but why not 100% more? Why not 1000%? How big is this market? Are you planning to go from 1% to 1.3% share? If so, what would it take to get to 5% or 10% share?

I often ask CEOs about their growth model: how fast can the company grow if they pull all the stops? Can the business start amping up and go asymptotic at some point? When? Rarely have they thought about their outer limits of growth. Considering how essential growth is for the valuation of a start-up, you'd think every board of directors would be asking these questions. Yet they rarely do, which further encourages an incremental mindset.

Even though our companies were hyper-fast growers, I still feel in hindsight that I could have done more to drive ambitious goals. I have never overdone it, but I surely have underdone it. It's so easy for any leader, including me, to retreat to seemingly safer and more achievable goals. It reminds me of Theodore Roosevelt's famous speech, "The Man in the Arena":

> The credit belongs to the man who is actually in the arena, whose face is marred by dust and sweat and blood; who strives valiantly; who errs, who comes short again and again, because there is no effort without error and shortcoming; but who does actually strive to do the deeds; who knows the great enthusiasms, the great devotions; who spends himself in a worthy cause; who at the best knows in the end the triumph of high achievement, and who at the worst, if he fails, at least fails while daring greatly, so that his place shall never be with those cold and timid souls who neither know victory nor defeat.

Why did eBay not become Amazon? Why did IBM not become Microsoft? Why didn't taxi companies invent Uber? Why didn't Hilton or Marriott invent Airbnb? Why didn't Oracle invent Snowflake? Why didn't BMC invent ServiceNow? Why didn't tape automation companies invent Data Domain? Why didn't Ford invent Tesla? The answer in all those examples, and many more, is incrementalism.

Teach your people to drive the business to the limits of its potential. So what if you don't get there? At least you went for it! Don't settle for respectable mediocrity; seek to exploit every ounce of potential you are entrusted with. If you want to win big, imagine a radically different future that is not tethered to the past. This is why innovation always seems to come from the least expected places. They don't have a past to care about. They have nothing to lose, no ships to burn behind them.

Tying These Battles Together: Using Audacious Goals to Outpace Your Competition

All our companies were radical departures from the past. In the disk backup business of Data Domain, we ended up competing with what were called "virtual tape libraries." Those were not actually tape libraries at all; they were arrays that put virtual tape images on disk. The "tape" was still the unit of management, even when we switched from physical tapes to disks. For a long time, customers would back up to disk yet still make a physical tape to be stored offsite. Old habits die hard, and incumbents fight against the tide for their survival. Data Domain replaced all of that with network replication, which eventually became the norm. A big goal, not an incremental goal.

ServiceNow entered a market against incumbents whose products were unpopular, aging, and rigid. It required deep, specialized, and scarce knowledge to upgrade these systems; making changes was too hard, too expensive, too risky. ServiceNow broke through that: it allowed modestly skilled IT people to manage, maintain, and change their systems on the fly, often several times a day instead of once every 18 months. This radical change endeared our platform to IT people all over the world. Its user-friendly, dynamic, and high-level architecture then spread to other service domains, which embraced ServiceNow with equal fervor.

Snowflake was also audacious from day one, reimagining data management for cloud computing. The founders were steeped in traditional database technologies but were bent on rethinking everything they could. They were driven by a sense of dissatisfaction with the state of the art, using a "clean sheet of paper" approach to many long-standing issues. Incumbents such as Teradata, Netezza, Oracle, and Microsoft had gradually been losing favor for analytically intense, highly scaled workloads. And although the public cloud wasn't new, it had never been exploited for both high performance and massive scale, which Snowflake offered customers.

The results were mesmerizing, often multiple orders of magnitude faster than the competition, both for the largest data generators and the smallest and least sophisticated of users. The founders also built the system to be highly self-managing and self-provisioning, reducing maintenance costs to our customers. Public cloud competitors with legacy architectures have struggled to compete with newcomers like Snowflake that produced radically different results.

As long as there are no new challengers with new ideas, you can do fine with an incremental approach. But in free markets, somebody is always thinking about dramatic changes. You're much better off doing so yourself rather than hoping it won't happen.

Another lesson from these examples: attacking markets that have weak, unpopular incumbents is infinitely easier than chasing strong, popular occupants. Customers do not easily part with products that do the job for them. They have enough on their plate already. You need massive, not marginal differentiation, or they will simply filter you out as noise. The incumbents sneered at ServiceNow and publicly ridiculed us instead of taking stock of the situation. Folks prefer narratives that make them feel safe, however removed from reality those narratives might be. Intellectual honesty is a frequent casualty in business.

Lead Your People into These Battles

Leaders have to channel the organization's state of mind. They make sure everybody is dialed in, talking about the same things, and feeling the same sense of discomfort and anticipation. In larger companies with many employees, it's easy to get out of alignment. Hordes of workers often have no real sense of what their company is up against. It is not their fault; it means senior management has distorted the landscape and left most of their people too far removed from the real action.

Even start-ups face this problem as they evolve. A very small, very focused team starts to add a person here, another there, until half the staff no longer understands the competitive landscape. Before long there's a reorganization that moves people around to new roles, which we used to call "same monkeys, different trees." Instead of anticipating what things should look like in 12 to 24 months, given the projected growth rate, people settle into status quo, business-as-usual mode. That's a big risk, unless you as the leader force everyone out of that mode.

Do an unsentimental evaluation of what resources and staff you have versus how much you really need. There is usually more performance and efficiency to be gained from your existing staff, before you take the path of least resistance—unplanned, incremental growth, leading to mediocrity and waste. One of your biggest responsibilities is to stop that incremental attitude in its tracks.

5

Put Execution Ahead of Strategy

Great Execution Is Rarer than Great Strategy

There are tons of articles and books on the topic of business strategy but relatively few on execution. That strikes me as remarkable because in practice it's hard to separate strategy from execution. When a business is struggling, how do you know if the problem was caused by a flawed strategy or poor execution? If you don't know how to execute, every strategy will fail, even the most promising ones. As one of my former bosses observed: "No strategy is better than its execution."

Still, most people prefer to discuss strategy rather than execution. Perhaps that's because they see the former as a more high-minded, intellectually stimulating subject, while they see the latter as boring and pedestrian, simply a matter of getting your hands dirty, working hard, and checking action items off to-do lists.

This is especially true in Silicon Valley, where strategic narratives are much treasured, widely discussed, and frequently rehashed.

But those folks actually have it backward. Strategy can't really be mastered until you know how to execute well. That's why execution must be your first priority as a leader. Worrying about your organization's strategy before your team is good at executing is pointless. Execution is hard, and great execution is scarce—which makes it another great source of competitive advantage.

In technology, and other sectors as well, we are overflowing with capital and interesting ideas. What we lack are people who excel at running with those ideas and making them real. Over the years I have been involved in numerous executive searches for different companies, which brought me face to face with the surprising dearth of execution talent out there. Silicon Valley is well populated with great engineering talent and people who know how to launch new products with small teams. But scaling up and running a disciplined and mature organization is a different matter.

Part of the problem is that there are endless books, videos, and courses on how to be an innovator, but very few on how to execute. Where would most start-up founders go to learn, assuming they even had an interest in the subject? This is why we often observe increasing dysfunction as organizations grow. I sometimes compare it to five-year-old kids playing soccer: a mob following the ball across the field in a clump, with nobody truly playing a position.

Treat Execution like a Teachable Competency

It's helpful to compare execution with sales. Both are absolutely essential components of any company's success. But only one of them is commonly given a systematic process to train new recruits in the fundamental skills they need.

It used to be a tradition for aspiring sales types to seek their first job with a large organization that ran an elaborate, weeks-long or even months-long sales academy for new recruits. Companies such as IBM and Xerox used to be great places to start a sales career, in part because of all that free training.

At Snowflake, we offer a clear career path and professional development for sales staff. We assign recent college graduates to follow up on inbound leads; their goal is to qualify and set meetings for our more senior salespeople. It's a hard job being on the phone all day, talking to strangers and trying to set up meetings, but it gives them a bedrock foundation for their sales skills. Next, a business development rep gets promoted to selling to smaller enterprises and institutions. Talented reps can then graduate to full-fledged enterprise sales. These are elite sales roles, highly compensated when done well. The final upward step is to our so-called Majors team, where dedicated account managers take care of our largest 200 accounts.

The idea is to take people from a relatively inexperienced station in life on a journey to become elite professionals in their field. Having the prospect of progressing through the ranks like this is a selling point in attracting the best, brightest, and most ambitious. Your entry-level job isn't just a job; it's the first step on a clearly defined career trajectory.

But there are fewer paths that systematically prepare young people for general management roles, where execution is the name of the game. And most people these days who aspire to be start-up founders or corporate CEOs aren't eager to wait around for training. They want to charge in headfirst, figuring things out on the fly. They can only hope not to do too much damage before they really know what they're doing.

New recruits also see their older colleagues entering very senior roles at ever-younger ages these days. It is not unusual now to see CEOs in their early to mid-30s. I have worked with many of these upstarts in an advisory capacity. They are smart, ambitious, hard-working, and driven—but many simply have never had a chance to observe excellent execution or an opportunity to make useful, educational mistakes. One of my favorite observations is that "good judgment comes from bad judgment." Experience may be overrated by some, but it's hard to find a substitute for it.

New managers have to learn from and through their management chain. When we promote inexperienced managers to senior roles, chaos ensues. It becomes the blind leading the blind. Organizations cannot scale and mature around inexperienced management staff.

At Data Domain, we built and sold an appliance, which was a completely integrated hardware and software solution. But we were all software guys with limited hardware backgrounds. We struggled in numerous ways for years until we finally landed on the correct leadership in contract manufacturing to lead us out of a never-ending sequence of reliability problems.

When I joined ServiceNow, the organization was quite immature in terms of management execution. The only way I knew how to solve that was from the top down, not the bottom up, and that is what we did. We also experienced severe service reliability problems because we lacked the management maturity in building and managing cloud infrastructure. It had to be solved from the top down, which we eventually did.

Joining Snowflake, the company had superlative ability in innovation through its founding ranks, but it lacked the ability to scale and mature. We solved that by hiring that exact skill and experience in new leadership. You need both innovation and discipline, or the place will simply implode on itself. The common mistake is relying on our innovators to also provide discipline. Those things rarely go hand in hand, if ever.

Getting Strategy Right

Even though it is widely overhyped, strategy obviously matters a great deal. You need to figure out what all the alternative approaches are and make hard decisions about why some make more sense than others. This exercise alone is worth your time and effort, as it expands the scope of your leadership team's discussions.

The problem with strategy development is that it is often reflexive, based on prior experiences and pattern matching at other companies. Jumping to conclusions without extensive reasoning, exploration, and discussion can have devastating consequences. It's also vitally important—yet very difficult—to maintain your intellectual honesty. Can you see things as they really are and fully appreciate what is happening? Human nature has a strong tendency to rationalize situations, to convince us that no significant changes are necessary. Reality can rattle us, making us nervous and uncomfortable. To cope with the stress, we talk ourselves into a less damning interpretation. This is why groupthink and confirmation bias are common and incredibly dangerous to the well-being of the enterprise. It is the role of leadership to maintain a culture of brutal honesty.

I've seen this phenomenon repeatedly in the much larger companies I've competed against. They usually failed to accurately assess the threat we posed to them, so they didn't begin to mobilize against us until it was way too late. For instance, EMC, in their desire to fight off Data Domain, kept buying companies and resold our competitors' products to neutralize Data Domain in their accounts. Eventually, EMC was forced to undertake an unsolicited takeover or risk Data Domain ending up in the hands of a much more formidable entity than we were at the time. They ended up spending billions of dollars to combat the threat because they were slow to fully recognize the significance of it. Luckily for EMC, it was not too late, just expensive.

At ServiceNow, one of our big competitors was BMC, whose CEO was once quoted as saying that they could "grab a few Java programmers and do what ServiceNow does on a Saturday afternoon." His denial of ServiceNow's appeal led to disastrous consequences.

It's hard enough to compete against a formidable opponent, but it's impossible if you can't even recognize your biggest threat. ServiceNow went on to become only the second company in history to exceed $1 billion in software-as-a-service revenues, while BMC was taken private by a private equity firm.

Snowflake's competitors, likewise, treated us for a long time as a cute, cuddly, little upstart, not a serious threat. We ended up leading an industry, while some of the largest companies in the world, after finally recognizing what we could do, have been rushing to catch up by trying to copy our offerings.

Treat every strategy with caution, and take care to avoid becoming intellectually or emotionally wedded to your preferred strategy. You may be horribly wrong and need to bail on it. As Scott McNealy famously said, "fail fast"—the sooner the better. We sometimes use the expression "that dog won't hunt"—not in reference to a person but to a strategic approach that just isn't working, no matter what we do. It's hard to say that if you're irrationally attached to a strategy.

Strategy Problems versus Execution Problems

In Silicon Valley, we often see start-ups struggle to make the most of their revenue opportunities and build momentum. Usually, the conclusion is that the VP of sales is underperforming and needs to be swapped out. The partners rarely entertain the possibility that the problem is the product, not the sales execution.

So how can you tell if your struggles are due to flawed strategy or weak execution? How do you know if your emotional impulses might be leading you astray? In my experience, most sales shortfalls reflect either an inadequate product or a disconnect between the product and the target market. In other words, what you're offering doesn't resonate with the people you expected to like it. A strong product will generate escape velocity and find its market, even with a mediocre sales team. But even a great sales team cannot fix or compensate for product problems.

There are real limits to what salespeople can and cannot work with. Likewise, if your product requires world-class execution in other departments, you are in trouble—because that kind of talent is in short supply.

Without strong execution, there is literally no way to know whether a strategy is failing. Eliminate execution as a potential factor first, and then move on to evaluating the strategy. Great execution cannot save a failing strategy, but it will help you decide more quickly whether it's time to change your strategy.

You Don't Need to Hire Consultants or Strategists

Many executives, especially at big companies, feel insecure about strategy and want to bring in consultants to inform and drive that aspect of the business. That's how firms such as McKinsey and Bain make a fortune. You can hire them to organize your data, generate pretty visualizations, write up a detailed analysis, and deliver a more eloquent articulation of your strategy than you could ever do by yourself. Plus, it might enhance your executive authority in board meetings if you present a strategy developed by a major consulting firm. Those people are experts and specialists, and have elite educations, so of course we can trust them, right?

You should resist this temptation by remembering an old joke: "Consultants are people who borrow your watch, tell you what time it is, and then keep the watch." In the long run, you are much better off working on your own strategy, without the fancy language and pretty slide deck. Develop confidence in your own authority, not somebody else's. Great operators live, breathe, and own their strategies.

Likewise, in many large companies, it's common to see dedicated strategy roles, often at the VP level. These people are basically in-house consultants because they have no operational responsibility. This alternative is at least cheaper than outsourcing strategy to expensive consultants but with the same fundamental disadvantage of separating strategy from execution. The people drawing the map will still be very different from the people driving the car, which creates a misalignment of incentives. The operators won't like simply being told what the strategy is.

The third option is the one I have always chosen: operators in charge of each business unit must also be the strategists for their business, and the chief executive officer must also act as the chief strategy officer. I trust executives with strategy more than so-called strategists because executives are informed by real-life dynamics. They are on the firing line, are responsible for results, and have to live with their choices. In contrast, pure strategists (either outsourced or internal) will be quick to blame the execution, because it is surely not their strategy that is lacking. If you can't trust one of your executives to set the strategy for his or her sphere of responsibility, all the consultants in the world can't fix that problem.

You will become a better strategist as your execution improves. Problems will seem less confusing, with fewer possible explanations for issues. More clarity will lead you to make better decisions, with less random guessing.

The bottom line is that great execution can make a moderately successful strategy go a long way, but poor execution will fail even the most brilliant strategy. That's why, in an amped up company, execution is king.

PART

III

Align Your People and Culture

6

Hire Drivers, Not Passengers, and Get the Wrong People off the Bus

Drivers Wanted

Years ago, when I was at Data Domain, we adopted a goal for recruiting that we only wanted drivers, not passengers. The slogan was based on a Volkswagen commercial at the time: "On the road of life there are passengers and there are drivers. Drivers wanted."

Passengers are people who don't mind simply being carried along by the company's momentum, offering little or no input, seemingly not caring much about the direction chosen by management. They are often pleasant, get along with everyone, attend meetings promptly, and generally do not stand out as troublemakers. They are often accepted into the fabric of the organization and stay there for many years.

The problem is that while passengers can often diagnose and articulate a problem quite well, they have no investment in solving it. They don't do the heavy lifting. They avoid taking strong

65

positions at the risk of being wrong about something. They can take any side of an issue, depending on how the prevailing winds are blowing. In large organizations especially, there are many places to hide without really being noticed.

Passengers are largely dead weight and can be an insidious threat to your culture and performance. They inadvertently undermine the mojo of the organization. They sap the animal instinct and spirits you need in business to thrive.

Drivers, on the other hand, get their satisfaction from making things happen, not blending in with the furniture. They feel a strong sense of ownership for their projects and teams and demand high standards from both themselves and others. They exude energy, urgency, ambition, even boldness. Faced with a challenge, they usually say, "Why not" rather than "That's impossible."

These qualities make drivers massively valuable. Finding, recruiting, rewarding, and retaining them should be among your top priorities. Recognize them privately and publicly, promote them, and elevate them as example of what others should aspire to. That will start waking up those who are merely along for the ride. Celebrate people who own their responsibilities, take and defend clear positions, argue for their preferred strategies, and seek to move the dial.

Making the Distinction

This distinction between drivers and passengers can be subtle to discern, and therein lies a problem. Few people are exclusively passengers or exclusively drivers 100% of the time. Most of us fall somewhere in the middle.

Whenever I bring up this notion of drivers vs. passengers at an all-hands meeting, I can see that it makes some people uncomfortable.

They may have never seriously considered the question in an objective and honest manner. At one such meeting, an engineer raised his hand during the Q&A session and asked innocently: "How do I know if I'm a driver or a passenger?" My flippant answer was that he'd better figure it out before I did. That was good for a few laughs, but the underlying message was that we need to ask more of ourselves so the answer will become self-evident. If you can't answer the question in an overwhelmingly positive manner, you are probably too much of a passenger.

This line of inquiry has other benefits. Employees should be able to look at themselves in the mirror and feel strongly that they matter to the organization, that they contribute in significant ways, that their absence would significantly hurt its results. If they can say those things honestly, they will feel far more secure and confident in their own value. It will also advance their careers at any company that recognizes and rewards drivers.

People who realize that they're mostly passengers have essentially two options. They can try to stick around without changing their pattern of behavior, which might be possible if they work for one of those large companies that spend decades decaying and declining before finally going out of business. On the other hand, when such a company is struggling, passengers are the first to be thrown overboard during a so-called reduction in force (RIF), better known as a mass layoff. It is not unusual to see organizations actually perk up after a RIF because all those passengers are no longer dead weight.

The better option for passengers, of course, is to start changing their ways by emulating drivers. In the long run, that's the only path to job security.

Getting the Wrong People off the Bus

When my core team joined ServiceNow, and again eight years later when we joined Snowflake, we knew we'd find problems. Otherwise their respective boards wouldn't have hired a new CEO. In such situations, at any level of a company, the first order of business is sorting out the valuable people from the deadweight (including but not exclusively those with a passenger attitude). Then you have to do what Jim Collins described in *Good to Great* as moving the wrong people off the bus and putting the right ones on the bus, in the right seats. In that order.

Parachuting into any new company or business unit is hard. Everybody is on edge, waiting to see what you're going to do. But you can't let their anxiety slow you down from immediately assessing your people. Don't surrender to the temptation to go into wait-and-see mode, hoping that time will reveal everyone's true value. You need to make things happen, not wait around and hope for the best. You have to practice sizing up people and situations with limited and imperfect information—because that is all you are ever going to get. At Snowflake, for example, we made all the staff changes we wanted to in just a few months. I may not have known every last detail about the individuals in question, but it wasn't hard to see which departments and functions were falling behind expectations.

If you don't act quickly to get the wrong people off the bus, you have no prayer of changing the overall trajectory. We often believe, naively, that we can coach struggling teammates to a better place. And sometimes we can, but those cases are rarer than we imagine. At a struggling company, you need to change things fast, which can only happen by switching out the people whose skills no longer fit the mission or perhaps never really did in the first place.

The other advantage of moving fast is that everyone who stays on the bus will know that you're dead serious about high standards.

The good ones will be energized by those standards. If others start looking for greener, less-demanding pastures because they don't want to meet those standards, that's fine too. I know this philosophy may come across as harsh. But what's even harsher is not doing the job you were hired to do as a leader. If you can't find the backbone to make necessary changes, you are holding everyone else back from reaching their full potential.

Leaders who do not act will soon find out that their leadership is in question. Everybody is watching: not just what you are doing but also what you are not doing.

Pulling the Trigger

When I first started managing people, removing people from their positions was considered a last resort. It was simply not done unless the situation was truly egregious. That was the staid, paternalistic culture of the times, when the general assumption was that anyone could be coached for better performance. If someone was still struggling after coaching, his or her manager often faced more blame than the employee. That created bad incentives to move people around to other departments, or to put them on long term "performance improvement plans" that kept kicking the can down the road. A deep reluctance to fire anyone is still common in many companies.

This is especially true in Europe, where the governments make it more expensive to let someone go, offloading more of the costs of unemployment insurance on companies. Those cost pressures give managers an incentive not to make changes. But even in Europe, the costs of not taking action, and continuing to preside over mediocrity, are far worse than the costs of fixing a bad hire.

Younger me was too timid when confronting these situations. I learned over time that I was too slow in pulling the trigger, as were many of my colleagues. Then I started moving faster to replace people who were badly suited for their roles. And often not even catastrophically bad, just worse than the caliber of people we knew we could hire to replace them. This process of systematically upgrading the talent at each key role is called "topgrading," a strategy developed by hiring expert Brad Smart. I've even told my boards that if they could find a better CEO than me, they should replace me too. Fair is fair, and I can't expect to be held to a lower standard of performance than anyone else.

Finding the Right People

Of course getting the wrong people off the bus is only half the challenge. The other half is finding and recruiting the right people for the right seats, which is much harder. This is not a process that can be rushed. The cost of a misfire in time, money, and reputation is huge.

Leaders are expected to have well-developed networks, the ability to recruit, and the sharp critical eye to judge talent. Here are my thoughts for building a strong talent posture.

Maintain an Active Recruiting Posture

It's hard to maintain an active recruiting posture. We recruit for a role, fill the position, check the box, and move on to other matters that demand our attention. But some of our hires do not pan out, get moved around or leave, and then we have to start all over again. That is often the reason why we tolerate mediocre performance—because it is so hard to relaunch a recruiting effort.

I would often ask, when traveling and meeting key managers, what would we do if we lost this person or other. The question would often result in blank stares or saying they would call HR for resumes. Instead, we want to always have a list of prioritized candidates for each critical role. Candidates we would seek to engage as needed. It starts with knowing who is who in the field, how well are they regarded, and keeping tabs on their ongoing status. Status is always changing of course, so it requires tracking candidates over time, checking in with them, having some sort of ongoing relationship until the time comes to actively engage.

Sometimes we engage regardless of immediate need when a strong candidate is what we call "loose in the socket" and might consider a move given the right circumstances. You can't wait till you have an acute need; that is a reactive posture. If you wait for a vacancy to open, you can only tap the then-current supply, which may be quite suboptimal. So create a vetted, prioritized list of possible candidates for each critical role you are responsible for. And make this part of a periodic check-in on the topic: review lists of candidates and their updated status as part of discussion on the performance and status of the people currently occupying these roles.

Do not rely on acute sourcing tactics such as recruiters and LinkedIn. You will only see the active job seekers, who are unlikely to be the candidates you really want. In high growth companies, functions and individuals can easily get overrun, as the expanding needs of the organization exceed their capacity. So you must staff ahead of need. Recruiting never stops.

Perform what we call active "calibration" sessions on critical positions in a group format. In these sessions, executives and managers present evaluations of their direct reports and seek feedback from the peer group outside their chain of command. The idea here is to discern if the manager's evaluation of the person in question is either shared, questioned, or outright challenged by the broader organization. These sessions identify a lack of management congruency on people issues if there is one, but they also serve as a catalyst to address budding or lingering performance gaps. Basically, they create clarity and prompt action on talent gaps.

Ultimately, leaders are only as good as the people they surround themselves with. Once you get good at both hiring and firing, you are well on your way to great results and a thriving career.

7

Build a Strong Culture

Culture Matters More than You Think

Few words invoke more variety of meaning than *culture*. What does it mean in the context of a business organization? For our purposes, it loosely defines the dominant and persistent patterns of behaviors, beliefs, norms, and values of a workplace community. Culture describes how people come together as a group on a day-to-day basis. Is yours respectful, fluid, engaging, constructive, demanding, urgent, creative? Or is it dragging, political, CYA, risk avoiding, and confrontational? Workplaces are capable of all of those and many more.

Culture matters more than you think, and it is not optional. A strong culture can greatly help organizations and become an enduring source of competitive advantage. But a weak culture can easily destroy organizations from within.

An important question here is to what aim do you direct your culture. All platitudes and high-minded principles aside, the culture needs to serve the mission of the enterprise. Sounds obvious? It isn't. Most enterprises aim for making employees feel good, secure, and safe in their roles. They are aiming for strong net promoter scores (NPS) on their employee surveys. Management is angling for kudos for their virtuous leadership style. While there is nothing wrong with good intentions, we need to align the culture with the mission.

High-growth enterprises are not easy places to live. The pressure is relentless. Performance is aggressively managed. There is no let up. I have seen employees depart after a short time because the intensity and pace just wasn't their cup of tea. Culture is not about making people feel good per se, it's about enabling the mission with the behaviors and values that serve that purpose. It's unlikely that a strong, effective, and mission-aligned culture will please everybody.

Culture needs to become a cohesive force in the enterprise. We need our best and brightest to wholeheartedly buy into the mission, as well as a culture that enables that. Cultures sort and sift between people who buy into it and those who do not. That's okay. One size doesn't have to fit all.

Like it or not, your company has a culture, whether or not you care about it or actively try to influence it. The people you hire bring elements of culture with them and influence the culture they enter, often unwittingly. It is essential that leaders grab ahold of it, and start driving it to a desired state. Culture can become a force multiplier, but it doesn't just happen with good intentions.

When not much is done to drive a cohesive, consistent culture across the organization, you end up with an amalgamation of different value systems across functions and geographies. Dominant personalities will set the tone in smaller subgroups. That's the pattern in places with a weak culture: lots of fiefdoms that spend their days fighting each other more than they fight the competition.

Culture can't wait because it's highly persistent over time. The earlier you start after assuming leadership, the more malleable your culture will be. In large companies that have been around for decades, it is near impossible to turn the tide. New leaders get brought in, but the culture ends up defeating their efforts because people cling to their old, familiar patterns.

On the flip side, culture can become a formidable driver of performance and differentiation. Many successful organizations rightfully point to their culture as a key source of that success. It's often the one differentiator that others can't copy. Your competitors can gain access to capital, hire away your talent, and steal your ideas, but they almost certainly can't replicate your culture.

The key to driving a consistent culture is not just having high-minded principles and values. Many leaders seem to think it's easy to assemble a committee, agree on a set of values, print up some posters, put them up everywhere around the office, and voilà, there is our culture. The problem is that people don't learn from posters. Like children and pets, they learn from consequences and the lack thereof. If you want to drive a more consistent set of behaviors, norms, and values, you have to focus on consistent and clearly defined consequences, day in and day out.

When you get it right, people will feel protective of the culture and call out deviations, peer to peer. That's the sign of a culture that's really pulsing through your organization.

Establishing Cultural Values at Data Domain

The advantage we had at Data Domain was that there were only 20+ people when I joined in 2003. It's so much easier to affect the culture at a small startup, before large-scale hiring and the consequent importation of values and behaviors. At a small start-up, everything is so tentative and formative that a lot of progress can be made quickly. In some ways, you are dealing with a mostly blank canvas.

When we arrived, Data Domain was mostly clean in terms of culture, meaning that there were few excesses in behavior. We had a strong sense of shared purpose, and efforts and behaviors were generally aligned to the company's mission.

We codified our desired values in an acronym to make them easier to communicate and remember – R-E-C-I-P-E:

R = Respect

E = Excellence

C = Customer

I = Integrity

P = Performance

E = Execution

Respect may be seen as mere common sense, but it's far from common in organizations. We didn't simply mean being courteous in personal interactions, although that is certainly a sign of respect. More broadly, it's about always engaging with people in a genuine manner. Be interested, be responsive, be helpful whenever possible. Never ignore someone who reaches out to you from a different part of the company. Don't sit on a colleague's email for days or weeks. Respect also includes vigilance against any discrimination or harassment on gender, racial, or ethnic grounds. Those cases were rare, but when they happened, we dealt with them swiftly and severely.

Excellence means that we were all trying to be great at everything we did, not just the engineers and salespeople who were most in the spotlight. If you were an HR person or an accountant, we still expected you to internalize our drive for excellence. It's not easy;

you have to work at pursuing excellence every day. It is easy to give lip service to this value but much harder for everyone to hold each other to high standards and not give a pass to mediocrity.

Customer is the center of everything. A lot of companies know that, but you'd be surprised at how many do not. It's another area that gets a lot of lip service, but people often don't act on the importance of customers when it truly matters. I always used strong language about our customers: we don't leave any of them behind, ever. We have their backs through thick and thin. Their outcomes are our outcomes. I urged our people to feel empowered to act forcefully on behalf of customers. Not just the big, strategic customers but all of them. No exceptions.

I've been in companies that thought employees should be number one because they reasoned that well-treated employees would therefore treat customers the best. Why be indirect about it? We don't have any reason to exist without our customers.

Integrity means that all our stakeholders could believe what we said and trust our commitments, with no exceptions. We have to not only be true to our word but also to the spirit of it. Once that is no longer an absolute, you have entered a slippery slope. Trust is the first victim of integrity violations, which set off a chain reaction of negative consequences. Life is much easier when all stakeholders believe you are telling the truth because you have been truthful at every turn previously.

Performance is something everybody claims to aspire to, but few do because it's hard to hold people and functions accountable and drive for consistently superlative results. Confronting a lack of performance is never fun, but has to be done at all levels of the organization—based on data and facts, not negative emotions. Accountability is uncomfortable because we all live with the anxiety of not being good enough and the anxiety of telling others they aren't good enough. But if you want a great company, you can't give out free passes for mediocrity. Good enough is never good enough.

Execution as a value is a nod to focusing *less* on strategy, *more* on execution. As we saw in a previous chapter, this is not a reflex in Silicon Valley, where strategy is continually discussed, but execution is generally undervalued. Any weakness in execution is often treated as merely a reason to revisit the strategy. We taught everyone that it's impossible to know how good a strategy is until you know how to execute.

At Data Domain, we saw many of our competitors second-guessing their strategy and tweaking their plans for no good reason. We left them behind at least in part because we didn't do that. We kept our heads down, trusted our strategy, and focused on getting better and better at executing it. It's hard to beat a well-executing organization, even if the strategy isn't perfect.

Culture at ServiceNow

We applied everything we had learned about culture at Data Domain to ServiceNow. While the RECIPE framework had worked for us, we didn't want to summarily impose it on a new company without an organic process. That would have created too much friction with the founding staff at ServiceNow, who were already viewing us as an invading force in the early days of our tenure.

What did survive was an unyielding, customer-centric, high-performance culture. ServiceNow had built an outstanding product and had a loyal following among its customers. Customers liked both the company and the product; quite a few of our customers eventually joined us as employees.

When I started to impose a performance-driven culture, it took some time for the staff to get used to. ServiceNow was a San

Diego–based company with a more laid-back lifestyle; when I first got there it felt more like Colorado than California. The company had a screaming need to amp up its talent and culture. We had no presence in Silicon Valley to tap into its much larger pool of technical talent—so we established one. The San Diego office always retained its own, unique identity, but it progressed considerably on the performance spectrum. It was not an either/or trade-off: they didn't have to trade in their San Diego culture to become a more serious, focused, performance-oriented organization. ServiceNow performed well over time—which helped convince everybody we were doing something, and maybe a lot of things, right.

Turning Around the Culture at Snowflake

My first week at Snowflake, I noticed manifestations of the previous leadership team's desired values, including posters on the wall. It made the company appear sincere, kind, and high-minded. But the reality was, at times and in certain places and departments, at odds with those values. Within days we began seeing glaring deviations from its principled mission statement and posters.

Culture doesn't just happen because of a CEO's declaration or because senior management exhibits the willingness to act on core values. It happens when most of the organization is willing to defend and promote those values and call out deviations on a day-to-day basis. That was not happening much at Snowflake when we arrived. People had retrenched into their functional silos. And despite notable exceptions, the leadership team did not get along.

In major sales regions, I discovered problematic subcultures, which led to widespread complaints on our Slack channels, with people sounding off in ways they would later regret.

Few in leadership roles at our location in San Mateo seemed to be aware this was going on. People go underground with their opinions and feelings. Obviously, there was widespread awareness in the ranks, but that did not percolate up to the people who could do something about it.

Once we started getting a glimpse of this, we pursued former employees—who had nothing to lose—to shed some light on what they had experienced. Active employees generally refused to speak out, terrified of their own leaders turning against them. They were sitting on valuable restricted stock, which they were not going to jeopardize by making trouble and potentially getting fired.

Salespeople in cities and regions talk all the time, across company lines. They have all worked together at one time or another. That's why salespeople *outside* the company were more aware of Snowflake's challenging sales culture than our own management. That is how I first became aware of the problems, via some of our former employees at ServiceNow who had heard the word on the street. This episode was regrettable for a company that had beautifully expressed values such as integrity always, make each other the best, and embrace each other's differences.

On the bright side, this situation created an opportunity to demonstrate serious consequences for gross violations of our values. It took some time to fully track all the trouble spots (which weren't all in one place), but we identified and parted company with sales execs who had crossed the lines of acceptable behavior.

My senior team didn't feel the need to revisit Snowflake's stated values. There was nothing wrong with the aspirations that the company had crafted before I arrived. The problem was the variance between the stated values and the actual culture. You only get the culture you desire if you actively pursue and enforce compliance.

Your Responsibility to Protect Your Culture

Outbreaks of bad culture can happen in isolated pockets of good companies.

Snowflake was a great company when we had our issues with those misbehaving sales managers. In such cases, I believe that people should be removed from their roles much more quickly for bad interpersonal behavior than for bad business performance. We will work with people to improve their underperformance if their values and character are clearly on board with our culture. But treating colleagues or customers badly is a sign of a much more fundamental problem, not an inadequate skill set that can be improved with coaching.

People who choose to disregard our values are tearing at the fabric of the culture, which affects everybody in the organization. Even those who have never interacted with X will hear through the grapevine that X is abusive, unscrupulous, dishonest, or whatever the problem might be. If such behavior goes unaddressed—or even worse, if it is rewarded with a promotion for delivering strong business results—people across the company will conclude that the values and the inspirational posters are bullshit. Everyone will know that the *real, unspoken* culture is "Do whatever you want, as long as you make your numbers."

That's the biggest reason why glaringly offensive behavior is cause for dismissal. Not just because we seek to root it out and help those who suffered from it but also because we need to signal to *every employee* how serious we are. Culture results from consequences, good and bad, as well as from the lack of consequences. If you want a strong culture, you will have to make hard decisions to let certain people go for the greater good. There's no way to avoid those cases.

One exception is when young, impressionable people fall under the influence of bosses who flagrantly disregard our values. It is not entirely their fault if they were merely following their boss's lead, so we sometimes give them an opportunity to reset their behavior for the future. Such leniency has worked enough times that we keep an eye out for these situations.

We spell out our cultural standards for all new employees as soon as they join us so they won't be able to say later that they weren't advised. If they want to work with us, they have to take our values as seriously as we do. If they can't agree to that, they should save everyone a lot of time and frustration and go somewhere else.

In many companies, when things are going well overall, people become more tolerant of bad behavior because, well, why mess with a good thing? It gets written off as growing pains, the inevitable by-product of torrid growth. That's an easy trap to fall into, so you have to remain vigilant against it.

As you evaluate your own culture, ask yourself a few key questions. When you talk to frontline employees, do they seem energized, or does it feel like everyone is swimming in glue? Do people have clarity of purpose and a sense of mission and ownership? Do they share the same big dreams of where the organization might be in a few years? Do most people execute with urgency and pep in their step? Do they consistently pursue high standards in projects, products, talent, everything?

If you succeed in building and protecting a strong culture, it will simultaneously attract people who admire the culture while repelling those who find it distasteful. That's an intentional feature, not a bug. The degree to which people embrace your culture will give you a huge indicator of who will help the organization reach its goals and who might be dragging you down.

8

Teach Everyone to Go Direct and Build Mutual Trust

The Dangers of Silos

Years ago at ServiceNow, I was recruiting a high-profile executive to be our VP of sales, or what we now call the chief revenue officer. During the interview I asked which team at his current company did he consider to be his primary team. Not surprisingly, his answer was his sales team. The answer I was hoping for, however, was his leadership peer group, meaning his counterparts in engineering, marketing, finance, services, and so on, because that's the team that really runs any company. The sales team by itself is a just one silo within the bigger organization.

Many companies are plagued by good execution within individual silos but terrible execution across silos. Everybody tries to stay within their own organizational lanes, including the leaders running those lanes. People get good at managing up and down the org chart of a single silo but flounder when problems require

83

cooperation across silos. Whenever a problem cuts across departments, people flag it for the head of their own department and ask him or her to take it up with the heads of the other departments. This creates more work for everyone and turns department heads into messengers. It's a tremendous blow to efficiency.

Perhaps even worse, expecting everyone to stay in their silos enforces rigid power structures and encourages leaders to hoard power within their fiefdoms. These organizations tend to become very political, with those on top of the silos enjoying great power while everyone else jockeys for position to influence their department heads. It also forces disputes up to the top of the hierarchy, which some leaders actually prefer, instead of getting them resolved on a lateral basis. Personally, I considered it a failure on my part if executives had to come to me to adjudicate.

Organizational structures are not sacrosanct. They're just a means of arranging the chain of command, which can become too broad and unfocused without a clear org chart. The paradox is that any business that's large enough to have functional silos must pull together as if these organizational delineations barely exist. If the leaders of each silo reinforce their isolation from each other, surely no one at lower levels of the organization will feel an incentive to change this aspect of the culture.

Too many managers and executives try to maintain a shield around their silo and require those inside to obtain permission to speak to anyone outside. These insecure control freaks are far more common than you might imagine. Fortunately, it's possible to redirect them.

A Better Option: Going Direct

We have a saying we often repeat at our companies: *Go direct*. If you have a problem that cuts across departments, figure out who in those other departments can most directly help you address the issue, and reach out without hesitation. Everybody, and we mean *everybody*, has permission to speak to anybody inside the company, for any reason, regardless of role, rank, or function. We want the organization to run on influence, not rank and title. We want everyone to think of the company as one big team, not a series of competing smaller teams.

We also expect that all attempts to contact another person will be acknowledged promptly and responded to thoughtfully. It is not acceptable to ignore a colleague just because you outrank someone or don't feel like dealing with their concerns. I have seen people coming from other companies act that way, and we correct such behavior the moment we become aware of it. To set an example, I personally respond to any employee who emails me. It might just be a brief sentence redirecting them to someone else, but they will get a reply.

It often takes a lot of communication and reinforcement to make going direct a core part of your culture. Our employees have heard me explain this concept numerous times, because the reflex to go vertical rather than horizontal is so strong. But if you as the leader keep stressing the importance of going direct, you can break everyone's habit of staying within silos. After a while, people will engage laterally just as easily as they do inside their own teams.

The same is true at the department head level. It has always been a priority for me to bring my department heads together and use them as the governing body of the company. My role as CEO is to facilitate their initiative and encourage them to reach creative solutions, not simply to tell them what to do. Everyone gets a seat at the table as we hash out challenging issues. Or in the age of remote work, everyone gets a square in the Zoom gallery.

This approach makes executives much more comfortable working directly with their counterparts, instead of sending problems up to my office for dispute resolution. My office is not the magic kingdom! My senior team has learned that they can save a lot of time and effort by going lateral instead of vertical. And that helps them set a good example for everyone else.

An opposition to pulling rank should include the CEO by the way. If I can't garner support for my position on the strength of my argument, I shouldn't win a dispute. You can win battles in the short term by flashing your badge and ordering people to give up, but in the long term that will cause more problems than it solves.

Building Trust

Going direct will only work as a strategy if your people default to trusting their colleagues in other departments, even though they don't have a direct reporting relationship with them. Trust is foundational to team effectiveness—it's impossible to overstate how important it is. Organizations where most people trust each other have a much higher quality of life than those who do not. They focus their energies more on the organization's priorities, rather than checking up on whether colleagues are doing what they're supposed to be doing or whether someone is out to sabotage them.

Trust never just happens—it needs to be earned and developed. Everyone has to aim for it and work on it constantly. Business affords constant opportunities to both earn and lose trust. People can detect an untrustworthy colleague quickly, almost by instinct. Most of us start off relationships with a show-me attitude, rather than blind trust, and a single disappointing experience can make it hard to recover. Once burnt, twice shy, as the saying goes.

Trust is not always an absolute, as if you either have it or you don't. Some people, teams, and departments are partially, tentatively trusted. Others you learn not to turn your back on, because they are clearly and actively at odds with your objectives.

In low-trust environments, people quickly learn to play defense. They craft their actions based on how vulnerable they feel against the indifference or outright sabotage of their colleagues. They may well survive that way, but the organization as a whole will struggle. We cannot succeed when everybody is preoccupied with their personal survival, not the company's.

My favorite framing of this idea is from Patrick Lencioni's book, *The Five Dysfunctions of a Team*, a conceptual framework we have used over the years to assess how functional we were as a team. The model from Lencioni's book is reprinted below.

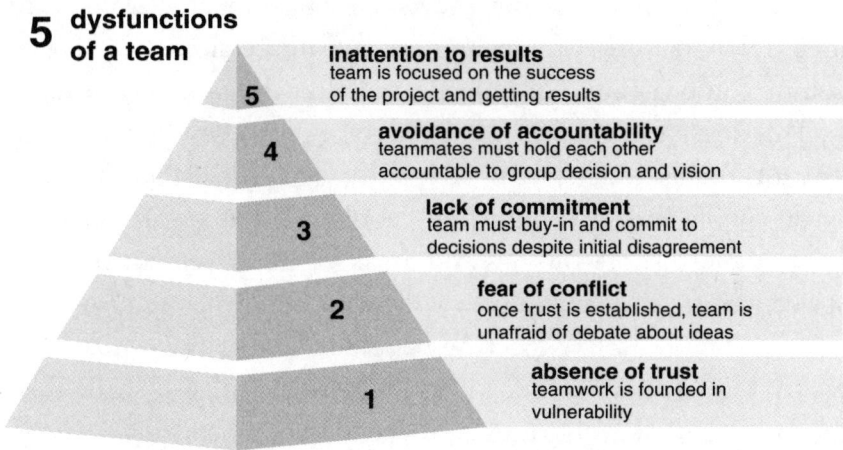

While there is a lot to this framework worthy of further consideration, the basis is trust. Without trust, all the other dysfunctions of a team—such as fear of conflict, lack of commitment, and avoidance of accountability—become difficult to address.

Are You a Trustworthy Leader?

To build trust in organizations, leaders must be trustworthy. You can't simply demand trust from anyone, including your direct reports. You have to earn it.

Each time I came in as a new CEO at three different companies, I could sense everyone's apprehension and lack of trust from day one. New leaders rarely seem to get the benefit of the doubt, regardless of their credentials or experience. People are naturally wary of change. But in time, trust can be earned by following through on your words and actions being consistent with your narratives.

People always monitor the variance between what you say and what you do—and especially how you treat the staff. They will detect the slightest patterns of misrepresentation, which, over time, convert to discounts on promises. This is why politicians have such low currency—most of what they say is disconnected from reality. They live in a world of appearances and impressions, where every promise can be delayed or fudged until after the next election.

This doesn't mean that you need to be perfect every time to garner trust. But as leaders, we need to offer up an honest accounting of our behavior. Trust goes up when people see that we are self-aware about our own shortcomings and areas for improvement. An honest accounting of your failures will work much better than denying those failures and expecting people to ignore them. Of course, this strategy will only work for so long. Trust will still shrivel up if you consistently fall short, even if you deliver a heartfelt mea culpa every time.

Hyperbolic projections will destroy any form of credibility and trust. So when you set expectations, make sure you have the resources and ability to adhere to them. Not just in terms of deliverables but also in how you treat people. For instance, if you say you have a zero-tolerance policy on an issue, don't make exceptions.

If you say you have somebody's back, then do. Words have consequences. People trust a straight shooter.

Even better, to truly inspire trust, underpromise and overdeliver.

Coming into Snowflake as CEO was turbulent. People weren't expecting it, the previous CEO was popular in the ranks, and I started making leadership changes almost immediately, which unsettled folks. At the first quarterly all-hands meeting I explained how, through proper focus and execution, not hoping and praying, the valuation of the company could reach 10x in a matter of 12–18 months. I saw plenty of disbelief in people's eyes that day, but we did end up taking the company public at 13–14x that day's number, and the stock doubled again on the first day of trading. I received many emails that week from employees, recalling that fateful day a year earlier when we made that 10x projection. One employee said in his note: "We didn't believe you that day, but you did exactly what you said you would do."

The Benefits of a High-Trust Environment

High-trust workplace cultures tend to correlate with high-performance organizations. In a high-trust team, people call each other out, without reservation, for the good of the business; no one feels put on the spot or made to look bad. If people can trust that everyone's motivations are honorable, not political, it allows them to focus on the problems and challenges of the business without getting defensive. People don't need to defend bad decisions in a high-trust environment. They can acknowledge a failure and move on quickly.

To set a good example, whenever I realized that one of my decisions had been incorrect and regrettable, I would publicly admit it and declare a fast failure. For instance, I struggled at Data Domain to build contract manufacturing excellence. We hired and ended up separating with a few leaders. I misfired on hiring, in part because I had never dealt with manufacturing before, being a software guy. I publicly acknowledged our failures but also said that I wouldn't stop until we got it right, which we eventually did.

We experienced an eerily similar situation at ServiceNow when trying to establish leadership for managing cloud computing infrastructure. This was also something I had not done before, and it was a new discipline altogether in the industry. We had well-publicized false starts on leadership in this area for which I took responsibility. As before, I told our people that we would not stop until we got to where we needed to be. Making mistakes is tolerable as long as you acknowledge it and seek to fully address the situation until you find the solution.

By declaring my own mistakes, I signaled to everyone that it was safe to admit their mistakes too, without fearing extreme consequences. No one gets everything right all the time. The faster we all face our demons and correct ourselves, the better off the business will be. But that can only happen in an environment of safety and trust.

PART

IV

Sharpen Your Focus

9

Put Analysis Before Solutions

The Problem of Racing to Solutions

The medical profession is "diagnosis centric" in the way it goes about treating conditions. This isn't surprising—how can anyone treat a patient effectively without a correct diagnosis, especially in the age of huge malpractice lawsuits? So doctors are trained to spend significant time running tests and eliminating possible causes. Only after a diagnosis is established can treatment protocols be implemented. And even then, doctors are taught to remain vigilant in case the treatment isn't working, which might signal a mistaken diagnosis. Life science is a murky business, and even the experts can't take anything for granted.

But business, I've found, has the opposite cultural tendency. We tend to be "solution centric"—we spend most of our time discussing solutions rather than diagnosing problems. We race to conclusions about what's wrong and what to do about it. We pattern match, reacting to situations based on our individual experience rather than studying the specific situation in front of us from a broader perspective.

It's easy to be irrationally confident in our judgment and anxious to move forward with implementing solutions. But if we are wrong in understanding the problem, our solutions won't work. For instance, my first employer, Burroughs Corporation in Detroit, one of the so-called B-U-N-C-H (abbreviation for Burroughs-UNIVAC-NCR-ControlData-Honeywell), concluded that the solution to their doldrums was to increase scale, which led to a merger of equals with Sperry UNIVAC. There is no compelling evidence that scale was what was lacking, seeing what has happened to UNISYS, the renamed entity that emerged from the merger, over the next 35 years. The challenges remained, just at a greater scale, as Sperry UNIVAC had its own issues. M&A (mergers & acquisitions) are often a preferred method of breaking out of an undesirable dynamic, but it rarely works out that way because the analysis of the problem is ill-fated.

Part of the problem is usually intellectual laziness. Your own frame of reference may lead you to a highly selective subset of the range of possible explanations. We're naturally drawn to certain narratives, and we resist others. Politics enters the equation when certain narratives make people look good or bad. Sometimes entire companies are prone to thinking in terms of well-worn patterns, and it's not expedient to deviate from the conventional wisdom. Winning the argument becomes more important than being correct in your analysis.

I worked for such a company in the mid-90s. My second major employer, Compuware of Farmington Hills, Michigan, wanted to break out of its mainframe-centric business. Mainframes were seen even then as legacy behemoths, and the cool stuff were minicomputers, the UNIX operating system, the desktop PC, and the Windows server. It wasn't even clear what, if any, problem the company was even seeking to solve. Mainframes were still an insanely profitable and highly predictable business compared to all the new technologies showing up in that era. Better yet, the mainframe business was about to massively reaccelerate due to the infamous Year 2000 (Y2K) glitch, just a few short years away. The company was trying to solve a problem that didn't exist, and it led to one ill-fated acquisition after another.

I ended up being assigned a leadership role in one of those acquisitions, the UNIFACE company in Amsterdam, the Netherlands. Numerous challenges came with this deal, not the least that the technology was already at the end of its useful life cycle, and things were only going to get harder. This deal didn't solve any problems, but it sure created many for years to come. Sometimes companies are so successful in their core business that they grow to believe that they can do no wrong and force their way into new ventures that are poorly analyzed and understood. As stable and enduring as the mainframe business was in those years, new technologies came and went at a furious pace. Almost anything you acquired in those years would have been short-lived.

Another cause of jumping to solutions is groupthink, which discourages new, creative, unexpected ways of thinking. We know from history that groupthink has led to disastrous outcomes, such the ill-fated Bay of Pigs invasion of Cuba in the early 1960s. Groupthink is innate in all human endeavors; the only question is how hard you work to be intellectually honest. Bias and prejudice are part of the human condition. So is confirmation bias, a newer psychological term to further describe these tendencies.

For instance, I recall a meeting at Snowflake early on to discuss the customer adoption of our Data Cloud. The proposals that day focused on a litany of initiatives to increase the variety and availability of data sources, assuming that was surely the reason that adoption was not as fast as we wanted it to be. Not a word of analysis on the nature of the problem or what all the possible explanations could be for sluggish adoption. To everybody's chagrin, I redirected the conversation to the nature of the problem rather than fast-track the proposals already presented. I am generally not a fan of just trying things, throwing ideas against the wall to see if they stick. We lose time and waste resources that way. Let's try a rifle shot instead of a scatter gun.

We have since that time massively increased the public availability of data resources, but we have also learned that not all data is created equal: some data sources are in high demand, while others get barely accessed. We started to get a glimpse of what we later referred to as data gravity, the idea that data concentrates in depth and scope around certain sectors. Instead of just brute force, a much more nuanced approach resulted from us actually understanding the early data cloud adoption challenges.

How to Focus on Analysis

So it behooves us to act more like doctors: slow down and critically examine situations and problems before settling on an explanation, never mind a solution. This requires intellectual honesty—the ability to stay rational and set aside our biases and past experiences. Consider the full range of possibilities, not just the first one that jumps out at you. Seek counsel outside of your direct environment.

How can you get good at doing rational analysis before jumping to conclusions and train your people to maintain intellectual honesty?

My preferred tactic is to start with so-called first principles. Break problems down into their most basic elements. Ignore what you think you already know, and imagine you are facing this kind of situation for the first time in your life. The more you have seen, the harder this tactic gets, but it's worth the effort.

In meetings, I often object to presentations where 90% of the content is about the solution, not the problem. My co-workers find it frustrating that I always want to walk back to the beginning rather than rubber stamp a program or project. They want to jump right into the action phase, so they see in-depth discussion about possible explanations as a waste of time. Of course, when you end up being wrong about the problem and therefore ineffective, that's a much more serious waste of time. Once you start examining and pulling a problem apart, the perspective often changes the range of possibilities. That often prevents a mistake that would have forced us to backtrack later on—wasting time, effort, and money in the process.

This brings me back to one of my favorite sayings, by Scott McNealy of Sun Microsystems: "Fail fast" (which I already mentioned in the "Getting Strategy Right" section in Chapter 5). If you find out that you were wrong, correct it immediately. Build a reputation as a rapid course corrector. You don't need to be right all the time to succeed if you can admit quickly when you're wrong. This will set you apart from the majority of people who get wedded to narratives too quickly and then refuse to revisit the analysis for fear of looking bad politically.

Analysis Is Especially Important for People Decisions

One area where this approach is particularly important is in hiring talent. Hiring decisions are naturally fraught with bias because so many human qualities are impossible to measure objectively. It's forgivable that some hiring decisions end up as failures, but what's not forgivable is refusing to recognize, acknowledge, and take action on hiring mistakes. Even after decades of experience, I have repeatedly hired executives who were successful in their past roles, well respected, well liked—and nevertheless turned out to be terrible hires. It happens to all of us!

How do you know if your analysis of a new hire was wrong? Several times a year we conduct what we call "calibration" sessions (which I already mentioned in Chapter 6), where each department head presents to their peers, profiling the performance and potential of their direct reports. The purpose is to highlight who we think are our ascending stars, who is struggling, and who is a serious concern. The department heads try to be as objective as possible, while relying on their peer group for a reality check on each assessment.

Any one of us individually might be biased, but the peer group is usually clear in its evaluation of talent. People end up either embraced or rejected by the peer group, with rarely much of a middle ground. In strong cultures, the managerial peer group can act like antibodies, rejecting a dangerous foreign substance before it can wreck the health of the organism.

These calibration sessions can be difficult, but they highlight any lack of congruence in the organization, if it exists. They also force us to face our demons: are we tolerating less-than-stellar performance in certain roles? Invariably that is the case to one degree or another. Could and should we aspire to do better? Analysis sharpens perceptions that tend to get dull in the daily hustle and bustle. Taking time out to explicitly discuss these topics can be invigorating.

Whenever there are glaring discrepancies in evaluating one of our executives, we double down on analysis rather than jumping to conclusions. There must be a reason why people are having very different experiences with this person. With enough time devoted to discussion, we always get to the bottom of it. Analysis first—especially when someone's future career is at stake.

10

Align Incentives
for Customer Success

Do You Need a Customer Success Department?

About ten years ago, it became fashionable in Silicon Valley to organize and staff a so-called "customer success" department. Suddenly it seemed like everybody had one, but they didn't exist much before then. The idea was to allocate resources for a dedicated team of people who would singularly focus on customer success.

Customers liked having a special team that would advocate on their behalf. These customer success folks would not report to sales or customer service, but they would coordinate and engage any and all resources of the company on behalf of the customer, to address whatever issues might come up. Typically, this team would be staffed with a blend of specialists from other departments, from technical to sales to product support.

Does that sound like a great managerial innovation? It certainly did to the folks at both ServiceNow and Snowflake, who had set up such functions before my arrival. They were happy to follow the trend set by other companies like ours. But not me. I pulled the plug on these customer success departments in both companies, reassigning the staff back to the departments where their expertise fit best.

Here's why I was so opposed: If you have a customer success department, that gives everyone else an incentive to stop worrying about how well our customers are thriving with our products and services. That sets up a disconnect that can create major problems down the road. People can become more focused on hitting the narrow goals of their silo rather than the broader and more important goal of customer satisfaction, which ultimately drives customer retention, word-of-mouth, profitability, and the long-term survival of the whole company.

For instance, at ServiceNow some of the customer success people grew quite dominant in the interaction with customers and coordinated all the resources of the company for the customers' benefit, including technical support, professional services, and even engineering. This had the effect that other departments sat back, became more passive, and felt less ownership of customer success. More daylight between the functions instead of less.

Customer Success Is Everyone's Business

The alternative strategy is to declare and constantly reinforce that customer success is the business of the entire company, not merely one department. This means that when a problem arises, every department has a responsibility to fix it. Everyone's incentives should be fully aligned with what's good for our customers.

If the basic functions of the company are working properly and are held to account, you won't need a separate department.

If your product is so bad that it requires an army of hand hold-ers, then apply extra resources to fix the product. And if there's a more garden-variety problem, urge everyone to take it seriously and address it directly. In any of those scenarios, creating a new depart-ment doesn't add any additional value. It just lets other departments that may have disappointed a customer off the hook.

The urge to rearrange people into new departments reminds me of the US government, where the proposed solution to every prob-lem is a new layer of bureaucracy. For instance, when the FBI, CIA, and Pentagon all failed to prevent the 9/11 attacks, none of them were truly held accountable. Instead, the government set up a mas-sive new cabinet-level organization, the Department of Homeland Security. No agency ever gets punished for failing to do its job; they all live to fight another day for more federal resources. Meanwhile a new organization just adds more complexity to the challenges of solving the underlying problem.

Customer grievances are best solved by establishing proper own-ership, reducing internal complexity, and removing bureaucratic intermediaries. The product developers and salespeople who work directly with a customer should never surrender responsibility for that customer's well-being, which directly affects their career pro-gress as well as the company's results. That way, everyone's incen-tives are aligned. It's even better if multiple departments overlap in terms of their scope so that no customer can fall through the cracks.

Here's an example of how this works in practice. At all three companies, we made our technical support people the organiza-tional owners of customer issues from end to end. We also moved technical support organizationally under the umbrella of engineer-ing, so they all reported up to the same executive, our head of engi-neering. It is not desirable in our experience when engineering is removed from, or does not feel the effects of, decisions by tech support. Engineering has de facto a support role: tech support has to work with the engineering department whenever they exhaust the limits of their own abilities. It is another form of organizational alignment.

While technical support owns customer issues, sales own the customer relationship, which cannot be relinquished to a customer success person. Our business is relationship oriented, not deal oriented or transactional. It is important that salespeople do not delegate part of their role to customer success types.

People will forget that you used to have a customer success department once the primary teams are fully empowered to solve problems on their own. You will end up with a simpler, less costly, and better functioning organization.

PART

V

Pick Up the Pace

11

Ramp Up Sales

Sales Growth Is About Timing

In my 2009 book, *Tape Sucks*, I wrote: "There comes a time when the venture must pivot from conserving resources to applying them rapidly, as fast as you know how to do effectively—when that cross-over time comes is not always obvious."

This is one of the questions I hear most often from entrepreneurs: How do you know when to ramp up a start-up's sales? There's no simple answer, but I can share some additional questions that should help you draw your own conclusions:

- Are you happy with your current sales productivity metrics? If not, how can you improve productivity before adding more sales headcount?
- Are you happy with the metrics of your lead generation pipeline? If not, how can you improve it?

- Are you being realistic in your timeline of sales targets? Are you projecting too much too soon, or too little too late?
- Are you being aggressive enough and thinking big enough to outpace your competition?
- Is your sales team buying into your targets and timeline? Are they owning the goals and fully committed to hitting them?

Trying to staff a whole sales team prematurely is a very common managerial mistake. So is failing to figure out what distinguishes top sales performers from weak performers before ramping up headcount. And so is hesitating to invest major resources to scale up your sales effort after all the conditions are in place. Here are three examples from my companies that will give you a better understanding of these common sales problems and how to solve them.

Data Domain: Don't Rush Sales Before You Cross the Chasm

At Data Domain, we didn't hire our first full-time salesperson until well into my tenure as CEO. First, we had to establish a good product-market fit before we could attempt to cross the proverbial chasm between early adopters and the mass market—a concept first described in Geoff Moore's book *Crossing the Chasm*. We weren't ready yet to establish a systemic, repeatable sales process that would yield consistent results.

The first salesperson we hired was technically knowledgeable and good at engaging with the technical experts at our potential customers. He knew the channel partners who could support and help us inside accounts, and he figured out the opportunities one at a time. Selling in these initial stages is more akin to business development than a defined, repeatable sales process. In a business development situation, every aspect is interpreted case by case, and we adapt to the circumstances at hand. Pricing and contract terms are flexible. Selling, by contrast, is a systemic, highly standardized process.

He was very successful and ended up staying with Data Domain for many years. But his style of slow, patient business development wasn't easy to replicate or scale. The second sales rep we hired didn't have the same set of skills, and failed. There was nothing wrong with him, but he fit a much more established, mature selling profile. We simply weren't ready yet for that kind of traditional salesperson. You can't brute-force a sales effort if the underlying conditions aren't in place yet.

Data Domain added salespeople at a very careful, gradual clip while we were upgrading our product to address an expanded market. We were quite limited in terms of performance and capacity in the early going, which constrained the number of situations in which we could viably sell. It took well over a year to staff to even a handful of sales heads.

But in the meantime, we also bootstrapped a well-resourced lead generation function. One big challenge of early-stage selling is insufficient demand, so we decided that we had to give our new reps a ton of leads they could follow up on, right away. A busy sales funnel boosts productivity and energy within a sales team, while allowing management to study the biggest sales challenges and see how the top performers are overcoming them. Conversely, if you skimp on resources for lead generation, your sales reps will end up having only a couple of meetings a week. That's demoralizing; they are literally dying on the vine. High levels of activity are essential to boosting morale and driving results.

Lead generation wasn't that expensive compared to the much bigger commitment of hiring and retaining direct sales staff. When a business is just getting off the ground, potential new sales reps will insist on guaranteed compensation plans, at least for the first year. So at one point, Data Domain had as many as three lead developers for every full-time sales rep. That is a ton of lead generation support. We weren't worried about scaling the sales effort yet; we were worried about crossing the chasm, becoming viable with staying power. The tactics we employed at such early stages are specific to the situation at the time and not meant to endure over time.

A few years later, with our product line more formidable, we stepped on the sales accelerator. We hired more reps based on the qualities we knew we needed, no longer just guessing who might do well. And we taught them a predictable, systematic process for making a compelling case to potential customers that would yield the envisioned sales productivity.

Our pivot from gradual, restrained hiring to opening the floodgate happened in a single quarter. It was such a dramatic change that our board members were stunned by how quickly we shifted the sales strategy and how well we executed it. The board had watched us for years as we had stressed caution and conserved our resources. But now we were doing the exact opposite: letting it rip.

This wasn't a hard call or a leap of faith. The numbers justified the pivot. If anything, we might have even pulled the trigger one or two quarters earlier. Because we waited until we had all the pieces in place, Data Domain's bigger, more ambitious sales force started paying for itself quickly.

Snowflake: Making Sense of Your Gunslingers and Flatliners

When I joined Snowflake, the company was growing fast, but it was costing us much more than a dollar in sales and marketing expenses to generate a dollar in revenue. The previous leadership team had been adding resources with a vengeance, but it was unclear at first why those extra resources weren't converting to results. Were we just terribly inefficient in selling?

As we started to drill down on this dynamic, it became clear that we had lots of "flatliners" on our global sales team—people who simply weren't closing deals or even building up their pipeline of prospects. Most of the company's growth was generated by a small group of "gunslingers" who delivered consistently strong sales productivity. So we knew this was an execution problem. If you can sell a product to companies in New York but not in Atlanta, the problem isn't your product. Clearly, something was wrong with how we went about running our sales effort.

It's quite common in early-stage companies for a small group of reps to be driving most of the revenue, while a larger group of flatliners are failing to contribute. The problem in these cases is usually a bad habit of hiring indiscriminately, and a lack of standardized, effective sales enablement. Sure enough, Snowflake had been growing its sales force so quickly that it had assigned people to open sales jobs without carefully or systematically figuring out what kinds of reps would do best in each role. Worse, we weren't giving our new reps nearly enough guidance about best practices to drive sales productivity. They were expected to somehow figure it out for themselves and magically deliver big numbers. It's no wonder some reps were off-the-charts successful because of the prior skills they had arrived with, while others were bottom-of-the-barrel, despite selling the same great product and drawing on the same level of marketing support.

Part of the problem was that Snowflake's recruiting had been mostly outsourced, a mistake for any sales organization in my view. If there is one skill a sales manager must have, it is recruiting. It has to be done in-house because recruiting is so core to successful sales management. Good sales managers are constantly hiring and firing, which helps them develop a clear sense of which candidates are likely to become gunslingers. They also understand the conditions that need to be met before another head can be added to staff. Sales managers will indicate where their next hires should land and which territories should they address. They are responsible for converting reps to productivity, so we follow their lead on where they want them.

After we stopped outsourcing our hiring function, taught our sales execs how to hire better, and improved our training in best practices, Snowflake's sales productivity began to broaden and climb significantly. We started hiring stronger candidates and giving them a proven, consistent path to productivity, rather than dropping them into the deep end of the pool, to sink or swim.

ServiceNow: Seizing the Right Moment to Ramp Up

In 2011, the year I joined, ServiceNow had a small sales team with off-the-charts productivity and accelerating sales per rep. The reps were proud of their success, full of energy and enthusiasm. The company ended that year with the same number of quota-carrying reps it had started with; any vacancies were filled, but no reps were added to the headcount. Nevertheless, the company nearly doubled its sales revenue that year, which I saw as a crystal clear sign that it was past time to ramp up sales. The company was starving for resources in other departments as well, but boosting sales and the sales-related functions had to be our top priority.

We backed up the truck and went on a massive hiring campaign to boost our capacity. The entire sales staff more than doubled in headcount in less than six months. It wasn't easy to recruit so many good people so quickly. We lured quite a few away from my former company, EMC, which ruffled a few feathers there.

Nothing is more indicative and predictive of sales results than quota deployed on the street. Quota is the level of sales dollars assigned to deployed sales representatives. Once they have a quota and they need to hit it to make a living, it becomes a steamroller of channeled human effort.

Here's a paradox of the ServiceNow example. In a static, low growth company, increasing sales productivity is viewed as a positive development. But in high-growth scenarios it's a negative metric because it means you aren't hiring fast enough. ServiceNow's sales productivity was too high when we got there. Our hiring spree caused productivity to level off for a few quarters. But that was fine, because our furious rate of staff growth would soon pay off with dramatic revenue growth.

Conclusion

Putting gasoline into a car's tank won't matter if the engine isn't working. Likewise, you can hire all the salespeople in the world, but they won't pay off until you've figured out your product, your market, your demand and lead generation systems, and the kinds of selling motions that will convert prospects to customers.

If you have a sales force that's stuck in the mud, don't just complain about the staff's failure to hit your targets and timeline. Ask lots of questions to figure out what's wrong. Then take bold steps to mitigate the problem as soon as you understand it. You can't simply take a "wait and see" posture while hoping the metrics will improve. You have to aggressively manage nonperformance, cut headcount if appropriate, or add headcount wherever you have the highest probability of converting sales potential to sales yield. Add headcount where managers have a record of converting them to yield and vice versa: do not add headcount to regions where things clearly are not figured out. That's hoping and praying, not sales management.

Equally important is making sure that your salespeople have the resources they need, including experienced and productive managers and colleagues. Never simply throw them into stone-cold territories without a viable plan or support. That's setting them up for failure, which will lead not only to their own failures but to *your* reputation as a leader who breeds failure. Word will get out, which will make hiring harder and set up a vicious circle of decline.

Don't let that happen. Set your people up for success, and watch them thrive.

12

Grow Fast or Die Slow

Why Focus on Growth?

"Grow Fast or Die Slow" is the title of a 2014 study by McKinsey & Co that examined thousands of software and services companies between 1980 and 2012. It concluded that growth trumps everything else as a driver and predictor of long-term success. "Super grower" companies, which McKinsey defined as 60% or more annual growth, had five times higher returns than medium growth companies (which had less than 20% annual growth). Super growers also had an eight times greater likelihood of reaching $1 billion in annual revenue.

The study found that when evaluating a young company, growth matters even more than profit margin or cost structure. Increases in growth drove twice as much valuation increase than equivalent improvements in profitability. No correlation was observed between cost structure and growth.

Wall Street has never needed a consultant's report to understand the magic of growth. Super growers are rewarded with rich valuation multiples, both before and after they go public. Since every business leader's job is to increase the value of the enterprise, you might assume they'd all be obsessed with growth. But you'd be wrong. Relatively few make growth as big a priority as it should be. Quite a few even seem content to remain slow growers. Why?

Two Problems: Uncertainty and Fear

One major reason is that too few leaders truly grasp the importance of growth. They have the misguided belief that their mission is to reach profitability as quickly as possible, and that growth can follow profitability. But that shows a misunderstanding of how value is created and investors think. Once a start-up begins showing profits, investors conclude that either it doesn't know how to invest in further growth or that it has run out of growth opportunities. They'll wonder why you aren't plowing those premature profits back into the business. They won't expect profitability yet; investors know that growth is a ferocious consumer of resources. That's what their money is for.

I have often distinguished between actual profitability and what we call "inherent profitability." Profitability is typically distorted in high-growth enterprises because so much of the current period costs is associated with future period revenue. The question is what would profitability look like if we substantially stopped investing for future periods altogether? Inherent profitability is driven by unit economics, or the gross margin line in the profit and loss statement. If things cost more than what we sell them for, the business will obviously never become profitable. The next question is how operating efficiency will benefit from increased scale. Those answers help us understand what the inherent profit-ability of the business really is.

For example, the general and administrative expenses may be as much as 20% or more of revenue in the early going, but as the business scales up, we would expect that number to start dropping below 10% of revenues. Not all spending scales linearly with revenues. Accounting can become the bastardization of economics when it obfuscates the inherent profitability of the business by focusing on current period income and expenses.

In my experience, anxiety about growth is a bigger problem than ignorance about growth. Leaders become afraid to burn too many resources or to make hard choices about where to invest their limited capital. Some are afraid that if the enterprise gets too big, they will lose control. Others are afraid that if they really go for it on growth, they may spin out and humiliate themselves. So they play it safe. But trying to hang on to a modest business doesn't mean you have a viable business. Your competitors will surely try to take those customers away from you.

When a business is struggling, it's only human nature to be afraid to admit failure and give up. You might tell yourself that a new VP of sales can solve the problem. Or your board might decide to appoint a new CEO. But the simple reality is that not all businesses are destined to succeed. The market will send clear signals if you are willing to hear them. Just because you might save a business doesn't mean that it's worth saving.

Slow-growing companies become the walking dead. Most would be better off failing catastrophically and quickly. At least with a quick demise, everybody can stop throwing good money after bad and move on to redeploy their human and financial resources to more promising ventures.

Silicon Valley is littered with companies lingering in the pro-verbial chasm for years and years. Their venture capitalists and management teams hope beyond hope that someday they will finally catch fire. I have personally been involved with more such ventures than I care to recall. Early on, in my naivete, I defaulted to inspecting their operational effectiveness. But that's like rearranging deck chairs on the Titanic; the ship will still go down unless it substantially alters course. In business that means confronting the question of commercial viability. For a business to break out and reach escape velocity, it needs a ton of differentiation. It needs to profoundly upset and disrupt the status quo. People yawn when offered merely marginal change.

Build a Growth Model That Stretches Your Goals

I often ask other CEOs to explain their growth model—in other words, how fast could their company grow if it optimally executed? What constraints would limit or enable their growth? Surprisingly, the response is often a blank stare. "Growth model? Not sure what you mean by that."

Sometimes they throw the question back at me. "How fast do you think we should grow?" Or perhaps, "We're on track for 30% growth this year. Do you think that's good enough?" How can I possibly answer those questions for someone else's business? The answers are relative and situational. For some companies in certain situations, 30% might be superlative, but for others it may be grossly underperforming. That's why you need a growth model—to understand the many factors that will enhance or limit your opportunities for growth.

It's often impossible to assess the true limits of growth. It's not just plugging numbers into a formula; it requires human judgment and insights. That's why we have to keep leaning into it. Both senior management meetings and board meetings should focus on challenging the assumptions that add up to the current growth model. Very often, challenging those assumptions will lead you to conclude that your growth target is too conservative. When in doubt, push the model to set a more ambitious target.

For instance, at Data Domain we initially set our growth targets conservatively because we were so afraid to get too far over our skis and lose credibility with our board of directors, a common sentiment among management teams. But this is the wrong instinct; I'd rather ratchet up growth expectations and fall short than not even reach for it. Behavior is informed, if not driven, by expectations. I recall a conversation with our sales leaders at Data Domain years ago discussing the next year's growth target. I wanted them to develop the target first so they would feel ownership of it versus having it imposed on them from on high. As we discussed their estimates, I asked what it would take to increase that initial estimate by, say, 25%. The team then rattled off a laundry list of things they had to do to get to the higher number. Well, why don't we just do that then? Goals are powerful: they change behavior.

When I first interviewed with the ServiceNow board in early 2011, they were understandably proud of the company's growth trajectory. When I asked if they could grow even faster, I received incredulous, if not irritated, looks in return. I didn't mean to act like a jerk; I just wanted to understand how they thought about growth. It can be an uncomfortable question, but it needs to be asked again and again.

You may find at some point that you are overspending on growth and investing ineffectively, but that's a rare situation. It's much more likely that you will get better and better at optimizing for higher growth rates and bigger goals. We can theorize all we want, but ultimately, we all learn best by doing. In my case, every company I led was a super grower, but in hindsight I could have productively applied even more resources, even more aggressively than I did. All my experiences have taught me that when in doubt, you should lean in and try to grow faster.

Leave the Competition Behind

Fast growth separates great companies from their competition. You can psychologically leave everyone else in the dust when you outstrip their growth rates by a considerable margin. It's intimidating and demoralizing to your rivals.

For instance, by 2007 Data Domain was leading a crowded market for deduplicating disk arrays and virtual tape libraries. Every disk storage company was competing for relationships with the original equipment manufacturers (OEMs) that sold the product to the ultimate customers, who were leery of start-ups for something as foundational as backup storage. OEMs were companies such as EMC, Hitachi, IBM, and NetApp. But Data Domain pursued a different strategy; we staffed our own direct selling organization. That was common in enterprise software (where many of us had started) but unorthodox in data storage.

Resellers would often pass on selling Data Domain because they were afraid of being muscled out by the big OEMs. Resellers were not going to jeopardize their lucrative franchises with the large OEMs to take on an upstart like Data Domain that represented a threat to the status quo. We ended up selling directly against the resellers, but after they started losing to us over and over, some started to come around. Customers started asking them for our product, so they really had little choice but to offer Data Domain. That's how a power dynamic changes; your leverage comes from having a strong product and a formidable ability to sell it. If possible, always own your distribution rather than delegate it to a third party. Nobody cares about selling your product more than you.

Our unorthodox decision to sell direct ultimately helped Data Domain dominate the market. It eventually reached fifteen times the valuation of its nearest competitor. Our zeal to beat EMC as the leviathan of the storage business was so strong that I personally went to Boston again and again to sell to prospects in their backyard. For businesses in New England, buying EMC was close to a religion, but we didn't let that deter us. We then started to hire away some of EMC best salespeople, who were tired of losing to Data Domain and open to a change. This shot across EMC's bow was even more demoralizing than losing some of their loyal customers. When you challenge very large companies, it helps to have a bit of a chip on your shoulder.

EMC tried everything possible to neutralize Data Domain's growth, including going after our customers the way we were going after theirs. But nothing worked—our growth momentum was already too strong. In the end they were forced to launch an unsolicited takeover to acquire Data Domain.

Continuing to Grow After You're Already Big

Growing is hard when you're a small start-up, but continuing to grow after you reach scale can be even harder. People naturally expect growth to slow when business gets to a certain scale. Don't give in to that assumption too quickly. Unlike the law of gravity, there's no law that momentum naturally has to slow as your revenues climb higher and higher. It's the size of your addressable market that dictates limits. Growth tends to slow down when you are starting to become well penetrated and saturated.

Many companies try to continue that momentum by investing heavily in a second major product or service—a sequel to whatever made them successful originally. But most have a hard time being serial innovators. They may stumble onto one great product and then assume that they can easily do it again. It takes intellectual honesty and humility to admit how big a confluence of factors gave rise to your original success. Just because you struck gold once doesn't mean you know how to do it at will.

A higher-probability path to growth at scale is to leverage your proven strengths to adapt your original offering for adjacent markets. Don't venture too far afield if you don't need to, though. You can expand your capacity to sell while at the same time increasing your addressable market—without trying to strike gold a second time. That's how we continued to grow ServiceNow, which was already a super grower when I joined but still had plenty of room to expand its core offering.

We got wind early on that human resources departments could really use a service management platform like ServiceNow, even though we had designed our product for people who run IT operations. We didn't speak the language of HR, let alone knew how to sell or market to HR professionals. But once we had an indication that this could be a huge market, we leaned into HR. We hired new salespeople who came from HR backgrounds and changed our terminology; for instance, what IT people call an "incident," HR people call a "case." Small changes like that were relatively easy at all levels, from product design to sales, marketing, and services. We created a separate business unit for HR so we could track its metrics separately. That unit became a stellar performer and still is to this day.

Emboldened, we then unleashed the ServiceNow platform on another half dozen new service domains, using our HR experience as a role model. We assumed that some of those additional experiments would fail, but they all caught fire. Our selling motion incorporated all these plays. We referred to it as "multiple clubs in the bag."

One business I resisted entering was customer support, which was quite far afield from where we were. Customer service centers are, by definition, much more consumer-driven than internal IT support, with much higher volumes of interactions. But one data point in favor of trying it was that we already used ServiceNow internally to handle support for our own customers, and it worked well for us. Despite my initial reluctance, I relented to the strong internal advocacy of several members of my leadership team, who turned out to be right. We built up our digital, end-to-end customer service offering into what we called "global business services."

All these different irons in the fire, all variations on our original offering, resulted in tremendous growth at scale, as well as a huge spike in our market cap. It took ServiceNow 12 years to get to $1 billion in revenues but only two additional years to get to $2 billion. Warren Buffett referred to this as the "snowball effect"—scale begets more scale. At $10 billion in revenue, if you can figure out how to grow by just 10%, you'll pick up another billion in a year.

Bringing Down the Costs of Growth

Snowflake was another super grower when I joined in 2019, closer to tripling than doubling its year-on-year revenues. Indications were that this was an incredibly compelling product in a market that really needed it. Demand was bottled up and frustrated by inadequate legacy platforms, and it was easy to show customers that we could offer dramatic improvement in their results. Basically, our salespeople had to say, "Try it; you'll like it." A combination of huge demand plus a compelling product gave us a perfect storm for further growth.

The growth challenge in this case was to sustain this hyperbolic trajectory at scale. While Snowflake was throwing massive fuel on the fire, its costs of sales and marketing still exceeded 100% of revenue. I know I said earlier that growth should be prioritized over profitability, but when it costs much more than a dollar to generate a dollar, you don't really have a business. This was not a problem we would naturally outgrow, as the company had believed previously. Instead, we focused on fixing the misallocation of resources, to make all this dramatic growth closer to profitable.

First, we needed to balance Snowflake's compensation plans with financial discipline. There is an organizational element to this: you simply cannot let your sales function run their own compensation plans. That's like letting the proverbial fox run the hen house. Compensation plans need to be precisely modeled against revenues to see what the effects will be at various levels of performance. Incentives also need to align with the company's objectives, not just the salesperson W-2. The company did not at that time permit multi-year contracts, something we changed almost immediately. Because of all these dynamics, we often oversold customers, contracting for more than they needed. Customers didn't care because they had a nominal cost rollover option from year to year. But this adversely affected our average discount, and hurt revenue in subsequent periods because customers were still loaded with capacity to process.

We also needed to balance contracts with consumption. Salespeople only cared about contract values because that's what they were paid on. But the company cared only about consumption because that's what translated to revenue. Bringing balance to that equation started to bring sales cost into alignment with revenues.

I cannot emphasize enough how important it is to have strong financial oversight and discipline on sales compensation. You may be tempted at some point to make your comp plans more generous to recruit and retain top sales talent, but abandoning financial rigor can be a fatal mistake—not just during the planning stages of each year but every day, literally from one sales deal to the next.

13

Stay Scrappy as You Scale Up

The Paradox of Scaling Up

One trap that leaders often fall into is failing to adjust to the natural life cycle of a company as it grows and evolves. If you try to run a mature, 500-person company like a 10-person start-up, you will almost certainly fail. But, paradoxically, if you lose all the scrappiness of a 10-person start-up, your mature company may never reach its full potential.

Let's look at the three main phases of a company's development and what's demanded of leadership at each stage.

The Embryonic Company

In the embryonic stage of a start-up, seed capital is applied to assess the feasibility of an idea, followed by subsequent rounds of funding to build the initial product. The team is usually a small, close-knit group who are laser-focused on building that first product. It has always amazed me how much can be accomplished with a founding team of fewer than a dozen people, often only a half dozen. You will never revisit those levels of productivity again.

At this point, the CEO job is more or less a part-time position for someone who is also the leader of a key function, such as technology or operations. Everyone is working, not managing. It's also not uncommon to see part-time outside CEOs, such as venture capital firm partners, because the demands on leadership aren't massive yet. At Data Domain, for instance, our principal founder, Dr. Kai Li, was the leader while the team was building the product, but he never even bothered to take the CEO title. He was assisted by our lead investors at two VC firms, NEA and Greylock. It wasn't until about 18 months after the company's founding that I was hired as Data Domain's first CEO.

The Formative Company

The formative stage starts when there is enough product to begin testing the market. You can finally connect with potential customers, letting them see, touch, and smell the product. You can get valuable feedback and experiment with pricing and support models. The goal at this stage is to find out if you really have a viable product or merely a technology in search of a problem to solve.

At this point the leadership challenge is bigger because you have to make huge decisions about how to price, position, sell, and promote your product. Headcount is starting to climb, which will introduce HR challenges. A rapid expansion of resources will accelerate your cash burn, often too quickly. As I noted in the chapter on ramping sales, there is no point in hiring ten salespeople when you don't yet know how to make even one salesperson productive. But with the lavish funding of start-ups over the past five years or so, spending restraints have gone out the window, often encouraged by board members and investors.

The formative stage is treacherous and the subject of much study and analysis by management experts. Notably, as previously mentioned, consultant Geoffrey Moore coined the term "crossing the chasm" back in 1991 to describe the unique challenges and activities associated with this phase of a start-up's evolution. Lots of companies make it far enough to attract some early adopters, and they have enough funding to pursue a much bigger market. But then they fall into the chasm between appealing to a narrow niche audience and building a large and sustainable customer base.

The key thing to remember is that you cannot brute force your way into any market. If you are met with lackluster response in the early going, it's time to go back to the drawing board, make sense of the feedback, and figure out your next set of moves. Trying to double down or triple down on spending to cross the chasm is a recipe for disaster.

The time to open the floodgates is when you have made it through the chasm and are confident that scaling up sales and marketing will convert a critical mass of new customers. Ironically, so many start-ups overspend dramatically during the formative stage, but then they're low on cash when they really need it in the next stage. You'll know when it's time to ramp up when customers are virtually ripping the product from your hands. If you feel overwhelmed by demand, you need to mentally adjust to the next stage of development.

The Scaled-Up Company

Scale is about maximizing growth by building repeatable, efficient processes and models of execution. We are no longer learning the basics; we have successfully reached adolescence, if not adulthood, and now we need to start acting like it.

For some companies, such as Data Domain, the formative stage takes years until the product improves enough to attract a large market. But because we had spent plenty of time to prepare for scale, our management team was solid, our culture was well established, and we were ready to throw the big switch and begin applying massive resources to fuel our growth.

For other companies, such as ServiceNow and Snowflake, the chasm was scarcely a speed bump. The products were so well fit to their respective markets that they saw rapid adoption almost from the beginning. Perhaps too quickly because the staffs of those companies were ill-prepared to enter the scaling-up stage. Both ServiceNow and Snowflake initially struggled to make this transition.

ServiceNow was still conserving resources when I joined, even though it had evidently crossed the chasm to viability. It was cash-positive and had banked significant cash from operations. But the company was literally choking itself by underfunding key functions. As I mentioned in the sales chapter, we had entered and exited that year with the exact same number of quota-carrying salespeople, even though the business had nearly doubled during the year. It was as if the company refused to move forward into the scaled-up stage.

Similarly, when I joined Snowflake, it was still behaving as if it was trying to survive the chasm, even though it had clearly exited the formative stage based on its meteoric growth and product acceptance. Spending was lavish and random. Even though we were burning $200 million a year in costs, Snowflake was still happily funding all-company ski trips to Lake Tahoe, as if we were still just a half dozen friends who could fit into a couple of cars. Operating efficiency and cash efficiency were dismal. There was no plan in place to scale operationally.

Sometimes the formative stage can be so enthralling that it's hard for leaders to move on. We don't want to let go of the romance and excitement of those early days. It's almost like wanting to keep hanging around your idyllic college campus after graduation instead of confronting the responsibilities of the real world.

I myself have been guilty of waiting too long to add essential resources. At Data Domain, I ran the company all the way up to a $50 million run rate before hiring a CFO. I used to hire senior executives sparingly back then, preferring to hire more lower-level people to do the work rather than senior people to oversee the work. That was clearly a mistake, as I realized once we brought on Mike Scarpelli as our first CFO. Until then I had no idea how much value a topflight finance chief could add! I later made sure to bring Mike with me as CFO (and my trusted partner) at our next two companies, ServiceNow and Snowflake.

Hang On to Your Early-Stage Dynamism

It's useful to distinguish between these stages of evolution because the operational modes are so different. Many leaders fail because they cling to old habits after they should have shifted gears. CEOs and boards need to be aware of the danger signs that a leadership team is stuck in an earlier stage of development.

In an embryonic start-up, you live hand to mouth; your instincts and reflexes are primal, almost like a wild animal. Whenever I hire someone at that stage, I look for direct impact, not some high-minded or abstract approach to business. But someone who excels at getting things done in an embryonic environment may struggle at a mature company, where there are lots of systems and meetings in place to slow down spontaneous, reflex-driven decisions.

Conversely, when you bring someone who has previously worked only for multibillion-dollar, steady-state companies into a start-up trying to cross the chasm, the mismatch can be epic. You might as well be on different planets. For instance, at ServiceNow I once hired an executive from a much larger company who came with good credentials. But he kept pushing to hire a massive staff for his department and launch huge programs, which was both inappropriate for our stage of development and completely unaffordable at that point.

We are all prisoners of our past to some extent. We bring our frame of reference, shaped by our unique combination of experiences, into any new role. But the most valuable leaders are those who can combine the scrappiness of a start-up leader with the organizational and diplomatic discipline needed in a big company. Those who can scale up or scale down as required. Those who can set aside their experience when necessary, apply first principles, and think through situations in their elementary form.

Most companies lose their original scrappiness as they get bigger. They lose the eye of the tiger, the instinct to focus relentlessly on the core drivers of the company's success. As they add more and more organizational layers and staff who are neither making nor selling the product, it gets easier to waste time on issues that have no line of sight with the company's mission. Too many strategists, too few hard-core doers. Distractions abound, to the point that some companies even lose sight of the customer.

Your mission as a leader is to figure out how to hang on to your early-stage dynamism and avoid the lethargy of mass and bulk. One technique I use is to challenge key people with this question: "If you could do just one thing for the remainder of the year, what would that be and why?" The reason is that as companies get bigger, they start advancing numerous initiatives simultaneously. Before they even realize it, people start moving like molasses and lose their sense of focus. Try to regain that by narrowing the aperture on priorities.

Similarly, I ask our teams what's the one thing we should be doing urgently that we are not doing for some reason? This is to avoid getting too engrossed in day-to-day activities and failing to see the forest for the trees. Always be paranoid about what you are not doing but should be. And, conversely, what are you doing that's of marginal value but crowding our more essential ways to use our time and resources?

For instance, in the early days of the pandemic many companies announced that they were suspending nonessential travel. Why did it take a global crisis for them to look closely at various practices and decide which ones had no significant impact? Any company that stays scrappy, at any size, will constantly be eliminating non-essentials of all sorts.

PART

VI

Transform Your Strategy

14

Materialize Your Opportunities— the Data Domain Growth Story

Much of our discussion so far has been about execution, especially developing an intense focus on the mission. But that doesn't mean that strategy doesn't play an exceedingly important role. Over the next three chapters, we'll see how strategic transformation played out at Data Domain, ServiceNow, and Snowflake.

Strategic Lessons from Data Domain

Our years at Data Domain yielded formative strategic learnings that had a major influence on our subsequent experiences at Service-Now and Snowflake.

Data Domain was a data storage company founded in 2001 that offered business customers an array that could filter out redundant data segments on the fly. In use cases such as data backup and recovery, it yielded extreme efficiency and speed compared to the tape libraries and automation systems that had previously dominated those markets. For example, a Data Domain array could hold 50 full backups in a storage space that would previously hold only one.

Tape technology went back all the way to the first days of computing. Tape drives were cheap compared to disk drives, and they had the advantage that a tape could be ejected from a drive, shipped offsite for safekeeping, and eventually recalled for recovery purposes. For decades the data security industry was composed of companies that made tapes, drives, loaders, and library storage and offered customers automation, logistics, shipping, and storing of tapes.

Then little Data Domain, with its war cry of "Tape sucks! Move on!" threatened to disrupt the whole ecosystem. People chuckled at this cheeky slogan, but our brash start-up mostly succeeded. Let's look at the reasons why.

Takeaway 1: Attack weakness, not strength.

Popular incumbents are hard to assail, but in this case, no one really liked tape automation systems. The IT people who made a living managing these systems were low-ranking professionals inside their companies, stuck with the technology equivalent of cleaning bathrooms. Not surprisingly, they were not enamored with their jobs. Half the time when they attempted a recovery, they could either not locate an entire or correct tape sequence or the tapes failed to load or had become unreadable. Our "Tape sucks" bumpers stickers were often plastered over tape library machines at data storage trade shows.

Takeaway 2: Either create a cost advantage or neutralize someone else's.

When businesses are making major purchase decisions, they usually don't care how their IT people feel about one product versus another. Economic imperatives rule.

Everybody knew the inherent advantages of mechanical disks: they were fast, reliable, and easy. Unfortunately, they were expensive. Tape held an insurmountable 10:1 cost advantage over the cheapest disk array at the time. But then Data Domain cracked the armor with its highly efficient, embedded, inline deduplication capability. Tape automation systems were usually backing up the same data, day in and day out, even when a customer had minimal changes from day to day. For example, a first backup maybe compressed at a rate of, say 70% or so, but the second backup would increment the storage footprint by only a few percentage points, if that much, because only the unique segments that were new from the previous day would be stored. Every subsequent daily backup would do the same thing: only marginally increase the storage footprint with segments that were new that day. That's why the deduplication technology pioneered by Data Domain was able to permanently alter the data backup and recovery landscape.

Because disks could drastically compress and deduplicate data, the cost advantage of tape systems evaporated, which overcame the only reason a customer might prefer tape.

Takeaway 3: It's much easier to attack an existing market than create a new one.

Creating so-called new categories out of thin air is a favorite cocktail party topic among marketers, but it doesn't happen that often. (Apple is often the exception, with category-defining innovations such as the iPod and iPad.) When a truly new market does appear, it's usually due to a confluence of industry-wide factors and circumstances, not the innovations of just one company.

Data Domain's opportunity was clearly defined; it consisted of the entire tape automation market, worth billions of dollars in annual spending. While our potential customers already had entrenched relationships with our competitors, we at least knew exactly who was making the data storage decisions at those companies and how much they were spending. In other words, we knew exactly which doors our sales reps should be knocking on, and those people were certain to understand what we were talking about. They wouldn't be an easy audience, but they were knowledgeable enough to give fair consideration to a potentially superior offering.

We tried to name this new storage category ourselves, but even as the lead dog in the emerging space, the market ignored our attempts to name the new category and ran in another direction. We had to run our hardest to stay ahead of the rapidly emerging shift to disks. Eventually, we did end up dominating the market, adopting the nomenclature that had already become mainstream.

Takeaway 4: Early adopters buy differently than later adopters.

The downside of any established market is the friction created when new ways of doing things challenge the comforting traditions that may stretch back for decades. Older, more conservative professionals in any field may fear that an upstart technology will threaten their job security and livelihoods. But more forward-looking (and often younger) professionals get excited by breakthrough innovation and can't wait to try it out. That's what drives the distinction between early adopters and late adopters, explained so brilliantly in Geoffrey Moore's landmark book, *Crossing the Chasm*. If you try to sell to both groups the same way, you are very likely to fail.

The key strategy is to aim for early adopters first because they (and their companies) are more comfortable with taking a risk on an exciting but still unproven technology. They are also astute evaluators of new technology, eager to change things for the better and then show off to their peers how cutting-edge they are.

Late adopters—a much bigger area under the bell curve—are motivated by minimizing risk as well as costs. They have no interest in being the first kid on the block with some cool new technology. The definition of crossing the chasm is building a beachhead of satisfied early adopters, who can then be used as examples to reassure late adopters. You have to make an irrefutable case that your new solution is both safe and cost-effective. That's when the broader market will become accessible to your pitch.

Takeaway 5: Stay close to home in the early going.

If you can't sell close to home, you will surely fail farther afield. The closer your early customers are, the more easily you can communicate with them and gather useful feedback. You can also swarm nearby customers with more resources and attention. That's why it's no accident that Silicon Valley companies are especially likely to launch close to home. Local tech companies are kindred spirits, tech savvy, and classic early adopters. They're also well connected and prone to talk to their friends and acquaintances at other companies.

Data Domain worked hard to build up a core of about 50 customers in Northern California before we tried to expand to more remote territories. Because we sold a physical disk array that had to be racked and configured onsite in a customer data center, we preferred staying within a 50-mile radius of our offices. We could simply drive to the customer with a unit in the trunk of a car. If the customer needed a unit swapped or a disk replaced, we could return quickly at any time.

Companies that try to sell nationally, or even internationally, right from the start often spread themselves too thin, creating serious strain on their operations.

Takeaway 6: Build the whole product or solve the whole problem as fast as you can.

If you offer a partial solution that requires your customers to seek the rest of the solution elsewhere, you are making it easy for a competitor to drive through the gap you left open. Try to deliver a complete solution so you won't be so vulnerable to displacement.

To materialize Data Domain's opportunity, our product had to scale from the largest to the smallest customers, not just operationally but also economically. We couldn't pull that off in the early years, but our strategy was maniacally focused on offering a more complete solution as quickly as possible. Our disk array was built as a file storage system, which made it harder for backup software products (sold by third parties) to drive our storage. Backup software was completely adapted to tape automation systems because everybody backed up to tape.

The tape mentality was so deeply ingrained that some companies built disk arrays that emulated tape libraries, known as virtual tape libraries (VTLs). Backup software could handle tape, or disks that emulated tape, but not disks that simply presented as disks. Another problem: many customers still wanted to make backup tapes that would be stored offsite in case of a fire, flood, or other disaster. Old habits die hard. You can recover from data corruption with a local backup, but any calamity that wipes out a whole data center would also destroy the backup systems. So people treated backup as a two-step process: make the backup every 24 hours, and then move it to a safe offsite location as fast as you can.

Data Domain pioneered a solution—network replication—that merged those two steps. An onsite backup (ideal for immediate recovery) was copied and moved across a network to another data center (for disaster recovery). Network replication benefitted even more from our product's deduplication efficiency because networks can only move small amounts of data at a time. By only transferring new and unique data segments since the previous day's backup, we were able to solve the whole problem and deny our competitors an opening. Data Domain started out with a limited product, but by systematically plugging gaps and holes, we became hard to assail.

Takeaway 7: Bet on the correct enabling technologies.

Data Domain had one super important advantage: It was built from the ground up with a clean sheet of paper, designed to do exactly what we intended. We wanted to focus more on storage rather than backup and recovery, which would appeal to customers because storage was the core technology while backup and recovery were just an application of that technology.

Our strategy relied on Intel microprocessors, which were developing fast in both price and performance. Disks, in contrast, were slow to improve performance because they're electromechanical devices. We knew it would be a losing strategy to try to compete on performance just by relying on improved disk performance. But those Intel CPUs evolved so fast over the years that Data Domain was eventually able to transmit deduplicated data faster than others could transmit raw data, duplicates and all.

Another key bet: We didn't want to build a virtual tape library interface, because we knew it was a short-term transition technology, but we offered VTLs anyway. We knew customers would eventually abandon these interfaces, but we needed to match our competitors who were offering VTLs.

Takeaway 8: Architecture is everything.

This one can get very techy, but we've seen it play out over and over at our companies. Think hard about the ideal architecture for your product before you launch.

Data Domain performed the process of deduplication "in-line," meaning that the system sorted duplicate segments prior to writing data to disk. This was incredibly hard to do at speed, which ended up being our ace in the hole. Our competitors were all offering deduplication as a post-process; first they would copy raw data to a disk, and then they would trigger a second process to eliminate redundancies. Aside from complexity and additional costs, there are only 24 hours in a day before a backup cycle starts again. With data volumes growing by leaps and bounds, this two-step process was likely to soon make two-step processes impossible within a single day.

Not only did Data Domain land data on disk already deduplicated, it also started replicating the backup offsite while the primary backup process was still in progress. The beauty of our software architecture allowed it to walk and chew gum at the same time. We came up with another marketing tagline to tout this advantage: "Get inline."

Takeaway 9: Prepare to transform your strategy sooner than you expect.

Just winning your market is not enough. How will you sustain your trajectory once you do? What will be your next act? How will you expand your addressable market? Will you even recognize the need to shift your strategy before you hit the proverbial wall?

There is always an awkward tension between executing your current business plan and plotting your subsequent strategic shift. If you're an amped-up CEO, like I was at Data Domain, you will have a hard time lifting your head up to entertain longer-range considerations, such as finding new addressable markets to sustain your growth. It's like trying to lay new track in front of a speeding locomotive—too hard to slow down.

While we were so busy building our product, selling to our customers, and fighting off the competition, I started having nagging concerns about our future. Still, I was unduly fixated on the play we were currently running and desperately trying not to fumble the ball. It wasn't just a matter of focus. The market we had succeeded in beyond our wildest expectations was landlocked, meaning that it had no easily accessed adjacencies. We had already invaded the easy adjacencies, such as network replication and disaster recovery.

We needed to get into backup software as a category because that was the software that drove our disk array. It would provide opportunities to further innovate, bringing backup software into the disk and network generation, tightly integrated with the disk array. We imagined we could easily double or triple our runway in this manner. We explored options to acquire backup software but could not find a suitable solution. The backup software companies were also coming our way, seeking to invade our markets. They saw the same opportunity that we did, but they were larger and better capitalized.

The other avenue we explored was to enter the primary data storage market. There were other ways to address data protection and disaster recovery than through backup software products, and some companies such as NetApp were already selling what they called snapshot solutions, which took a snapshot of a data volume and used it as a backup copy.

Data Domain executed extremely well on its core business, and we fought off the largest data storage companies in the world as they tried to slow us down at every turn. But as busy as we were stretching our lead, I did not pay enough attention to the larger strategic context. As the market developed rapidly, incumbents reacted to the shift in technology, and every tape library and disk array manufacturer got in the game as well. They all tried to leverage their existing products, technologies, and incumbency against us.

The End of the Data Domain Story

Ultimately, we had the right ideas to expand beyond our core market but could not execute on them. Data Domain was acquired by EMC after a bidding war against NetApp in 2009. EMC was a strong suitor because they already owned backup software and were the largest data storage company in the world. Data Domain massively expanded once it had the benefit of additional resources under the EMC umbrella, which proved our thesis. Today, as a part of Dell Technologies, Data Domain still represents a multi-billion-dollar business.

As successful as Data Domain was, its inability to transform strategically has troubled me ever since. The issues we faced in scope, expansion, and runway now preoccupy my thinking. As a leader, you need to make time to assess these issues from day one; don't wait for the crush of urgent business to calm down.

I likely would not have joined ServiceNow had I not seen a much larger opportunity than the one the company represented at the time. That's the subject of our next chapter.

15

Open the Aperture—the ServiceNow Expansion Story

My Introduction to ServiceNow

Coming off the Data Domain experience, I kept reflecting on the strategic challenges we had faced and what we could have or should have done differently. The sale to EMC was a great outcome by any economic standard, but a CEO can't help thinking he or she aborted the mission when a company gets sold. (I had never sold a company before, or since.)

All of this influenced my perspective on ServiceNow as I began the interview process to become their CEO in early 2011. Since 2004, ServiceNow had racked up quite a growth record under its founder and first CEO, Fred Luddy. The company had only consumed a nominal amount of capital, was cashflow positive, and was close to doubling on an annual basis.

The founder and many of the early employees had hailed from another high-flying San Diego company, Peregrine Systems, which had also made a business out of IT service management software. Peregrine Systems went bankrupt in 2003, a rarity in the world of software, and ServiceNow was like a Phoenix rising from its ashes. It offered a huge improvement on the legacy installed base of existing service management software products.

At first, I didn't know much about service management software, more popularly referred to as "helpdesk management software" or "ticketing systems." Any time a user logged a request or an incident, the system issued a tracking ID as a virtual ticket. I wasn't super excited about this category, and neither were the analysts and pundits of the software industry. It was viewed as a sleepy, boring category. One analyst referred to it as the "last battle," suggesting that the category would soon cease to exist altogether. But after a closer look, four factors piqued my interest.

How to Spot a Potential Super-Grower

First, I was stunned by ServiceNow's extraordinary growth rate as of 2011. Something rare and special must be going on when a company can rack up such huge gains year after year.

Second, the incumbents in this market, HP and BMC, were not popular with customers. Their products were aging, architecturally deficient, complicated, and hard to support. If you recall one of the takeaways from the previous chapter, it's always better to attack weakness rather than strength. ServiceNow seemed to have a golden opportunity to capture the customers of these unpopular incumbents.

I remember conversations later on with executives at several large institutions who were literally pleading for the chance to replace their old ticketing systems with ServiceNow. We simply weren't ready yet for their scale of operation, but they wanted us to try anyway. Knowing that this intensity of demand was almost unprecedented, we never walked away from any project, however daunting.

The third factor that elevated my interest was a conversation with founder Fred Luddy, who revealed that ServiceNow was starting to be used for completely different use cases, beyond IT service management. Human resources departments and event managers had discovered and liked the software. This meant that it had the makings of a generic workflow platform that could address any service domain. Customers saw something that software analysts and industry pundits didn't: This was a platform, not a tool. A tool is a one-trick pony, but a platform is broadly capable of many different uses.

This really mattered because I dreaded a repeat of the Data Domain scenario, where a market eventually reaches saturation and there are no obvious ways to expand and sustain the growth trajectory. I never wanted to repeat that sensation of being landlocked. As a CEO candidate I had only sketchy evidence and glimpses of ServiceNow's future potential, but those signs were encouraging.

Finally, the company's venture investor showed me the highlights of a transcript of every conversation the VC firm had had with customers over the previous year. This is fairly standard operating procedure for investor due diligence. It was about a 60-page document, packed from top to bottom with enthusiastic quotes and comments. Customers not only loved the product, but they also loved ServiceNow's people. It's rare to read such superlative and consistent praise about a company.

Whenever you make a major career decision, it's impossible to know everything, but I now knew enough about ServiceNow. I was all in. There were numerous operational challenges ahead, but the fundamentals I saw in 2011 would hold up spectacularly over the decade that followed.

Improving Execution of the Original Strategy

In the early years of my tenure as CEO, we focused relentlessly on execution, not strategy. There was nothing inherently wrong with the current strategy, but we weren't yet close to executing it to its full potential. Finance was starving the company for resources, sales couldn't recruit to hiring targets, our cloud service was highly unreliable, and our engineering department was anemic in terms of resourcing.

As a helpdesk management replacement offering, ServiceNow had many of the same advantages as Data Domain. We were not creating a brand-new category, just a much-improved way of doing things. Our potential new customers had a clearly identified buying center with a budget, relevant expertise, openness to switching, and curiosity about what we could offer them. It wasn't hard for our reps to get meetings or bring potential customers to our live demonstrations. The contrast between what they already had and what ServiceNow could give them was glaring.

ServiceNow was more elegant and simpler to use than any incumbent, while solving their most vexing problems. The system was dynamic: non-programmer types could change database structures, workflows, reports, notifications, and even the appearances of forms that were used by IT people to create incidents and other IT tasks. This was entirely novel compared to legacy systems. Moderately technical IT people could now make changes on a daily basis, something completely unheard of in this class of software at the time. Before ServiceNow, changes to these systems were sporadic, if not nonexistent: too difficult, expensive, risky, and time consuming.

We did lots of deals, but they weren't large because we were only licensing the product to people who staffed the IT helpdesk. Furthermore, our feature set was limited to a few core modules of the IT infrastructure library (ITIL) framework, the industry standard for service management. In other words, we were not licensing enough users or giving them enough functionality. Adding more of both became the underpinning of the company's growth model in the first few years of my tenure.

Expanding Our Opportunities

As we fought through these early challenges, new strategic opportunities started to come into focus. Our first foray into what I call "opening the aperture" was to position ServiceNow as the "ERP for IT." ERP is an industry acronym for "enterprise resource planning." IT had never previously been what we call "platformed"—in other words, it had no all-encompassing management platform. Companies ran their IT functions piecemeal, via spreadsheets and email.

Our idea was provocative but not entirely credible because we still lacked many features and functions to make the idea of an ERP for IT a reality. We had a blueprint for adding the missing parts of our framework and test versions for some of them (such as the Configuration Management Database, a system to store hardware and software specification records) but not yet a finished, mature, and ready-for-prime-time solution.

Once we convinced IT executives that their entire IT staffs should be licensed on this system, rather than just the people staffing their helpdesk, our market grew by orders of magnitude. So did our deal sizes. Our argument was simple: this product isn't just for helpdesk people resolving incidents; it's also for network engineers, system admins, database administrators, and application developers. They're all integral to the workflow, and ServiceNow can improve the quality and velocity of every stage of the workflow. The help-desk people were routing the incoming requests and following up on status, but the actual work was being done by other experts who needed to be full participants on our platform.

We ran hard for years to fill in the blanks, gradually substituting all the placeholders with real products and turning the vision into a complete reality. Customers liked our strategy, even when they knew it still had a way to go. Our platform created a rich framework for numerous other functions and modules. It was a canvas that we could continue to add more innovations to in the future.

One of the more vexing challenges was to get our own people to move beyond their original mentality of merely building tools for helpdesk staffers. Some of our sales reps were happy and comfortable selling to a narrow niche of customers, and they wondered why we were pursuing a broader strategy. I tried to convince everyone that going bigger was the only path to long-term success. I started using expressions such as "Desk"—short for helpdesk—"is a four-letter word" and "Tools are for fools." The team had to embrace and master our positioning as a platform, which would make us so much more valuable than a supplier of tools.

Going Public and Going beyond IT

When we took ServiceNow public in June 2012, the perception of our constrained market opportunity limited the value of our IPO. Many investors simply did not believe this company had legs. Gartner Group was hosting so-called fireside chats during our IPO roadshow, telling investors that our entire addressable market totaled just $1.5 billion. That was very frustrating—how could anyone expect a company to trade at a valuation larger than its entire market? I can only chuckle in retrospect, after ServiceNow became one of the largest, fastest-growing software companies in history, with a market capitalization well over $100 billion. This is why you should never put too much stock in the opinions of pundits.

By 2015, in addition to building out the main IT platform as described above, we opened the aperture even further by expanding into new markets that had nothing to do with IT management. Most notably, as I described a few chapters ago, we found a very receptive market in HR departments that need help addressing employee questions and problems. We also moved into cybersecurity, which combines security and IT professionals into a single workflow.

I personally resisted adding customer service support, which is a very different business—consumer-oriented, high volume, and unlike any of the other domains we were pursuing. I thought it was a bridge too far, but because we were already using ServiceNow internally for our own customer support, we had strong internal advocates for adding it as another new market. I eventually relented and gave the green light, and it turned out that I had been wrong. Our platform also worked great for consumer-facing customer service.

We started referring to our strategy as "global business services"—basically a single digital platform for all service domains. You no longer needed to know how to navigate an organization to get your problems solved or questions answered. Service domains became digital experiences. For example, instead of calling or walking over to the HR department, as employees did in the past, they now logged on to internal HR web pages that served as a comprehensive resource for HR tasks, information, questions, and issues. There they could find answers as well as create tasks and other units of work for the HR department to respond to and follow up on.

As I mentioned in the growth chapter, we fired up a series of new business units in pursuit of these new use cases and markets. We didn't expect them all to catch fire, but most did, and all of them persevered. To this day, ServiceNow continues to grow fast—and at considerable scale—by continuing to expand into new adjacencies.

Surviving the Competition

Our lingering paranoia from the Data Domain days led us to over-achieve on growth and expansion at ServiceNow. We never wanted to be caught again in the strategic dilemma of running out of markets. And it's a good thing that we treated "opening the aperture" as such a high priority because competitors such as Atlassian, Zendesk, Cherwell, and numerous others came after us with a vengeance.

One strategic threat was Salesforce, which had made it clear that they viewed our foray into what they called "the service cloud" as an act of war. Once our positioning became broader than other firms in the helpdesk ticketing space, Salesforce saw us as more of a threat. We were bringing the IT service model to new domains that Salesforce was also pursuing. Our mantra—"Customer service is a team sport"—encouraged companies to add relevant participants into our workflow. Bringing all relevant participants into a single workflow became our hallmark differentiator against traditional competitors. Other vendors trained their systems on the service department itself, leaving out the other departments that had to contribute to the resolution of an incident, problem, or task.

In retrospect, our strategy built a formidable moat against our competitors who wanted to enter the service management business. Many of them thought they could build a respectable helpdesk or service management product to compete with ServiceNow. But they didn't realize that ServiceNow derived its high functioning from all the other value-added modules and subsystems. It took a lot more than a helpdesk to take on ServiceNow.

That's how we found the breathing room to consolidate and strengthen our position for the long haul. Ultimately the real question isn't how broadly you can expand—it's whether you can hang on to the new markets that you expand into.

16

Swing for the Fences—the Snowflake Growth Story

Plan the Next Shift Before You Think You Need To

When I joined Snowflake in April 2019, it faced significant operational challenges but also tremendous opportunities. In this third case study of strategic transformation, I will review how the company evolved from its initial positioning to the more expansive trajectory we subsequently embarked on. We've seen how important it was for both Data Domain and ServiceNow to expand their addressable markets; Snowflake faced a similar challenge, just in the context of different issues and circumstances.

I arrived thinking that we had plenty of time to prepare for the future because the company was experiencing robust growth. But as time unfolded, it became clear that the strategic moves we started making early on weren't merely getting a jump on future opportunities. They were actually barely in time and far more essential than I'd realized.

151

This illustrates an axiom of strategy development: you need to think well ahead of the current dynamic in your market. If you wait until the need for a strategic shift becomes overwhelmingly evident, you may be too late to address it. Anticipating how markets—and your position in them—will evolve is absolutely essential. Nothing stays the same, even when you do nothing. Taking comfort in a favorable status quo may prevent you from ever moving significantly forward.

"The Data Warehouse Built for the Cloud"

Snowflake's original positioning, when it burst onto the scene in 2015, was that of a data warehouse, similar in concept to those offered by Teradata, Netezza, Oracle, and Microsoft, but one uniquely built for the cloud computing environments of the likes of Amazon Web Services and Microsoft Azure. Snowflake specifically offered to replace existing data workload platforms with a better architecture that enabled huge performance gains over what customers were then experiencing. At the time, businesses were struggling with workload capacity and performance constraints on their legacy data platforms, which were running in their own onsite data centers.

This pitch had both positive and negative connotations. On one hand, Snowflake quickly became associated with a recognizable segment of the market, which greatly facilitated its sales and marketing efforts. Potential customers understood what it was trying to do, and there was a clearly defined set of decision makers at key enterprises and institutions who might be persuaded to switch to a new data warehouse.

But on the downside, as Snowflake's brand became identified with data warehousing, it started to confine the company's market opportunities. And it couldn't help but get tainted with the broad brush of data warehousing's perceived limitations, even though Snowflake had broken through these shortcomings in spectacular fashion.

It would have been easy to stick to what had worked so well thus far. But we were at risk of becoming a victim of our own wildly successful positioning, which inadvertently linked us to a limited definition of our market, stuck in the status quo of data warehousing. We needed a more forward-looking brand, commensurate with our wide-ranging platform capabilities, which now went far beyond basic data warehousing.

It was heartening that our forward-thinking customers encouraged us to think beyond the status quo. They wanted to do as much as possible on the Snowflake platform, including mixed workloads that combined operational and transactional data processing capabilities. They did not want to spread their data across multiple platforms, which would aggravate data governance and the so-called siloing of data and add operational complexity.

Enter the Data Cloud

In late 2019 we launched a new strategy that we called the "Data Cloud." While we had no plans to stop offering data warehouse services, which had served us so well, the Data Cloud would expand our customers' operational capabilities and address the workload-related shortcomings of the legacy data warehouse. Traditional data warehouse platforms were single cluster architectures, which greatly hampered their ability to run concurrent workloads against the same data. They could not scale storage and computing power independently of one another. Snowflake did all this effortlessly, which massively expanded its scope and appeal.

Superlative workload performance had first attracted customers to Snowflake. But another major selling point was Snowflake's ability to "federate" data, meaning that when you had a Snowflake account, you could blend and overlay data from any other shared account. Snowflake was built from the ground up to be a data sharing platform; anyone with an account could plug into this massive data universe called the Data Cloud. There would be no friction, as data didn't need to be copied or replicated, and no latency because Snowflake queried the original source data, not a copy or derivative. When the source changed, anything that referenced that data also changed at the same time.

This was pioneering because data storage and computing had yet to migrate to cloud systems. Technology had already evolved to offer businesses massive infrastructure clouds such as Amazon Web Services and Microsoft Azure and application clouds such as Salesforce, Workday, and ServiceNow. But for most companies, data was still widely dispersed, fragmented, and hard to combine. Bits of key information still lived in millions of places, including the personal computers of individual employees.

That status quo made corporate chief information officers crazy. As data workload requirements kept growing bigger and more complex, the piecemeal treatment of data became more and more of a headache for them, if not a total nightmare. Data silos needed to be eliminated, or else data science would be impeded at every turn and its promise would largely go unrealized. That made our pitch for the Data Cloud compelling.

Going Even Broader: Data Marketplaces and Programmability

The next sector for Snowflake's growth, beyond the Data Cloud, was the notion of a "data marketplace" that would give customers a way to search, browse, discover, explore, and test new data being offered by other parties. A data marketplace would bring together the supply and demand for all sorts of industry-specific information, such as economic, demographic, supply chain, and industry-specific data. It would make it easy for companies that collected and analyzed data to promote their wares to a targeted audience and then do deals with the ease of a consumption utility model. Customers could pay only for what they used, without the hassle of a license or the long-term commitment of a subscription.

For instance, if your consumer goods start-up wanted mailing addresses for every married couple in Wichita, Kansas, a consumer data purveyor could produce that list and attribute it directly from their Snowflake account to yours, quickly and easily. This process of "enriching" data by adding attributes from other sources became a central focus across industries.

The Data Cloud has been further expanded with the addition of what we call programmability, meaning that software code processes data within the Snowflake platform itself. This expands Snowflake's scope into a data applications platform. It's a natural evolution of the Data Cloud that will further expand the reach and service the Snowflake platform can provide to enterprises and institutions everywhere. Our strategy built on successive layers of value: once the Data Cloud took shape and more and more data entered its orbit, the more compelling it became for software developers to access that live, rich data universe for their own purposes.

Playing Your Strategic Cards

Running a company is somewhat like playing a hand in poker. You may or may not be dealt good cards, but what matters even more is understanding the potential of the cards you were dealt. They will dictate your strategic options—whether you should call, raise, or fold at every round of the hand.

Snowflake could have easily stuck to its guns, pursuing data warehousing workloads as its core and only business. Had we played our cards that way, the perception of our value and potential would have remained a fraction of what they eventually became.

As you decide how to play your own cards, remember that it's not simply a matter of how large your current addressable market is. Sure, bigger is better, much better. But the question is how big your market will be in a few years. When external circumstances change, companies that run out of potential new markets to grow into are often forced into acquisitions or other desperate measures.

One solution may be to reframe your market as a subset of a larger market. For instance, the desktop computer market has shrunk to almost nothing, but desktop makers that expanded successfully into laptops and tablets have been thriving. The overall computing category is much broader now. Likewise, we expect data warehousing to end up as a subset of the much broader category of cloud data operations.

This is what ServiceNow did to the helpdesk and service management markets. People are no longer buying help desk or service management as stand-alone products. The definitions are much broader now, including operations and asset management, configuration management, and many other service domains.

That's why it was so important for Snowflake to evolve, reposition itself, and begin playing for much larger stakes. The challenges were profound for our engineering teams (who had to resource a much more ambitious agenda of projects) as well as our sales and marketing people (who had to substantially evolve their marketing and selling motions).

As you confront similar situations, remember that the sooner you lay the groundwork for expanding into new markets, the easier all these challenges will be.

PART
VII
The Amped-Up Leader

17

Amp Up Your Career

You Are a Product

Are you happy with your upward progress in your career? Could you go faster? Probably. Most people manage their careers in a haphazard fashion, jumping from role to role as new opportunities pop up. Being more purposeful about your career can amp up your forward momentum. As a CEO who has hired thousands of people into very successful companies, I've seen plenty of careers take off but also a fair number of them go sideways. The most common reasons for career stagnation (or worse, self-destruction) can be instructive.

As professional people, we are products. So try to product-manage yourself. Develop your product through education, training, and experience. Your resume is your shingle. Buff and polish it. Make sure it carries some punch.

In this marketplace, the question isn't whether you're qualified; it's whether you're *better* qualified than other candidates. What makes for a desirable, compelling product? Or better yet, a mind-blowing one? Here are my observations on the things you can do that will have the biggest impact on your career trajectory.

Education Matters Some . . .

A rigorous academic education is necessary to develop literacy, numeracy, and general capacities to learn, observe, and analyze. Employers need that foundation and typically require a four-year degree. It's hard to enter the professional workplace without one, although some have and do fine. But this degree usually doesn't need to be from an elite, Ivy League, or otherwise name brand school. There are some exceptions, a few industries that really care about the snob appeal of your diploma, such as investment banking, venture capital, and management consulting. But most employers don't care much about how highly your school is ranked. Elite graduates cost more, and most companies would rather do without the stereotypical attitude of their graduates.

It's popular to go back to get an MBA after a few years in the workplace. Many folks find themselves in the career doldrums and think an MBA might be the ticket to busting out. The business schools desperately want you to believe that. Yes, an MBA from a good university looks good on a resume. But there can be a huge opportunity cost to getting an MBA and not only in the salary you'd be giving up for two years. Your time away from your field will put you behind on experience compared to your peers.

. . . But Experience Matters More

The longer you are out of school, the more employers will favor meaningful experience over more education. The question becomes what did you do with that education? After 10+ years, most will hardly care at all about an MBA. Grad students are much less attractive than people who can point to a record of tangible achievements at a company. So think twice before pulling the trigger to get any kind of master's degree.

Build your record of accomplishments thoughtfully. Having a bunch of roles on your resume without clear success at each one can become a strike against you. You start to look like a passenger, not a driver. Avoid having a series of short-tenured jobs on your resume, especially if you can't name specific accomplishments at each one. It is hard to lay real tracks at any workplace in just 12-to-18-month stints. You may be unhappy and frustrated in your current role, but try to stick around long enough to make something of it.

Several short tenures in a row also imply that you had poor judgment in choosing those roles or perhaps that you're the kind of person who gets into chronic conflicts with management. One brief tenure will be seen as a fluke by future employers, but a series of them will be seen as a red flag. The shortest tenure I ever had was three years; all of my others were in the five-to-seven-year range.

Experience can be a proxy for aptitude but not a perfect one. People that have been with successful companies are often swept along in the vortex of the company's momentum. The aura of a great company can rub off on its employees, to the point that it can be hard to separate the company's success from the employee's. We've mistakenly hired some passengers this way, thinking they were drivers.

Conversely, I'm always intrigued by candidates who once crashed and burned with a company and learned something from facing those serious challenges. Humans always learn more from our struggles and failures than from our easy successes. Your experience will only be valuable to prospective employers if it taught you useful lessons that you can take into your next role. Speak credibly and insightfully, in detail, about your experiences, no matter how disappointing they were.

Aptitude Matters Most

Aptitudes are your God-given talents, whatever you are innately good at. Employers can give you experience, but they can't give you aptitude. Experience can help reveal your aptitudes, but hiring managers often don't try hard enough to understand and discern them. People literally never asked me in interviews what I thought I was good at. But that's always one of the first and most interesting questions I ask from the other side of the desk.

If you are light on experience for a role you want, redirect the conversation to aptitudes. Why would you be great in this position? Smart managers will usually pick someone with less experience but more aptitude. But bad managers become hung up on checking off the boxes on experience, in a futile attempt to minimize career risk to themselves. They make safe choices, not optimal ones.

The inverse of your strengths are your weaknesses. Are you self-aware enough to speak thoughtfully about your limitations? Everybody has them, but people are naturally reticent to discuss them. They think any interview question about weaknesses is a trap. But good managers know it's impressive when people are confident enough to be candid. Self-awareness is compelling.

Whenever talent is in short supply, as it almost always is in Silicon Valley, betting on aptitude is a great recruiting strategy for employers, albeit a less certain one. You can hire people ahead of their own development curve and inspire them to grow into challenging new roles.

Personality Tips the Scales

An energetic, engaging personality goes a long way in the workplace, as it does in every sphere of our culture. In politics, for instance, credentials seem to be completely subordinated by personality. It can sometimes compensate for lesser credentials, though less so in technical fields such as engineering and finance. But since everybody works in teams to one extent or another, the ability to collaborate as a team player is always at a premium.

We interviewed a sales rep years ago for a territory we were not yet ready to open up. As we were about to tell this candidate that we probably wouldn't have an opening anytime soon, he said that he had to get the job now. He said his wife had told him not to come home without the job! How could we say no to that kind of energy? We hired him immediately, and he became a successful sales rep. Personality tips the scales.

As you think about which aspects of your personality to put front and center, be mindful of the culture you are trying to join. A person who may be a great fit in one place may be a terrible match in another. When you're interviewed for a job, some of the best questions you can ask are, What types of people succeed best in this company? And which do not? And why?

Many years ago I interviewed for a general manager role at a large software company. My credentials for the role were appropriate, but the company foresaw trouble with my intense, hard-charging style, so they rejected me. As frustrating as that was, I later realized that they were right. I would have been unhappy, if not ineffective, in that low-key culture. But the same traits that made my personality ill-suited for that company also made me a better fit for start-ups, turnarounds, and scale-ups (i.e., very high growth ventures).

Start-ups typically need hard drivers, passionate leaders, goal-oriented and achievement-focused personalities—the kind of people who are easily frustrated in larger, more rigid, slower to evolve enterprises. We often liked people with a chip on their shoulder, who had a lot to prove to themselves and others. But it is easy to see how others would be less enamored by such personalities.

A big red flag in many workplace cultures is a sense of entitlement. We always sought low maintenance, low drama personalities. We valued traits such as strong task ownership, a sense of urgency, and a "no excuses" mentality. People who get things done rather than explain why they can't. This personality type lines up with our obsession with hiring drivers rather than passengers, as we saw in an earlier chapter.

Personality in hiring is a tricky subject because the standard advice is, "Be yourself, don't pretend to be something you're not." And that's true up to a point, but you have to speak persuasively about yourself, as if describing another person. It's not easy to position and articulate your "product" effectively, so it's worth practicing. Authenticity and sincerity are highly compelling traits, but that doesn't mean you can just wing it.

Hiring decisions are always fraught with risk and uncertainty. Like every experienced leader, I have hired extremely well-credentialed people who crashed and burned in short order. That's why many hiring managers will trust their gut instinct on someone light on experience but strong on aptitude and potential. In those situations, personality often breaks the tie. We have found that people who are hungry, humble, and express a "can't fail" level of determination are often a good bet.

Develop Your Communication Skills

One often-neglected skill set that can boost your career is your ability to communicate well, in both speaking and writing. How many rambling, poorly composed emails do you see these days? How many take you through the confusion and hell of the writer's mind? How many announcements do you read that bury the real news below several paragraphs of throat-clearing trivia?

An efficient, get-to-the-point writing style will help you at every stage of your career. Don't say, "I'm just not a good writer"—you can develop these skills. There are plenty of books, audio programs, and classes about effective business writing. Since I'm not a native English speaker, I had to work on this for years. I know it's possible to improve significantly.

The spoken word is another big deal for anyone on the management track. Your career can easily stall out if you can't speak well, or at least competently, in front of groups large and small. Many of us start out terrified of public speaking; the only way to get over that fear is to do it. And not just once in a rare while but as often as possible, ideally several times a week. You will get over your fears and get better at connecting with an audience. Eventually you will even relish those opportunities.

It helps a ton to be authoritative on your subject, to know exactly what message you are conveying and why. Beyond those basic requirements, try to develop a style that's authentic to you. A style that makes you feel comfortable and even powerful on stage. That can take years of experimentation, but it's worth the ongoing effort.

My style evolved into a conversational mode, as if I'm just chatting and telling stories to a couple of people in my office, rather than in front of hundreds. I start with the messages I want to convey and then fold in stories to illustrate my assertions. Stories are easy to digest, fun to tell, and often what the audience remembers most clearly. Start a running list of useful anecdotes, and keep adding new ones so your material doesn't get stale. You can also safely inject humor into your stories. And whatever you do, never read text bullets verbatim from a PowerPoint slide—that's the fastest way to lose everyone's attention. I've found that slides work best as visual aids for the audience, never as a crutch for the presenter. One way to do that is eliminate text bullets altogether, and amp up the visuals.

Hold On to Your Long-Term Goals

Most people embark on a career with only the foggiest notion of what their ultimate goal is. What do you want to be when you grow up? Resumes often reflect job-to-job opportunism and look like random walks. The choices we make along the way can be hard to rationalize in hindsight.

Having an endgame in mind will help you play a short game *and* a long game simultaneously. If you study the bios of successful people you admire, you'll see how each short-term job move helped set up bigger moves in the future. Each role gives you an opportunity to develop new mentoring relationships with people who inspire you and to bolster your network of peers. So you should evaluate each potential new role based on what it can do for you in the long run, not just immediate benefits such as salary, location, a prestigious title, or where your friends are working.

I've met people who knew they wanted to be a CEO when they were five years old, but I'm not suggesting that you be that obsessed. You can change your mind at any time about your long-term goals, and many do. But always think about your career over the long haul, and make decisions from that perspective. Clarity of purpose is extremely powerful.

Do Not Unduly Focus on Title and Pay

This follows naturally from long-term focus. In the first ten or so years out of college, don't worry too much about your salary or job title. Those years are all about building a strong foundation to launch your career. A fancy title and big paycheck won't help in the long run if you're not in a good role at a good company in a good industry.

Location used to be a huge factor but has diminished in importance under the influence of remote work and video conferencing. I was in Michigan for ten years pursuing a career in tech, when I should have gone straight to the San Francisco Bay area. My geographic mistake held me back enormously. Had I desired a career in automotive, I would have been in the right place, but my destination was tech.

Second, join good companies that have a mature management infrastructure. I usually advise new grads to avoid start-ups because you may observe and learn the worst habits there. Start-ups can be incredibly immature, filled with people who don't behave with professional decorum. In Silicon Valley they call it "lacking adult supervision." Early on you want to focus on getting a wide education in your field and laying a foundation for future leadership. Both are hard at a start-up, so don't get too enamored with the allure of hitting a home run via stock options early on.

You will have numerous jobs, titles, and pay grades over your career, not just between companies but within companies. At each step, be thoughtful and purposeful rather than opportunistic. Sometimes it might be best to take a step backward in title or pay to set up a better path forward. Your peer group will try to influence your career decisions, but be your own person. Steer your own ship. Never put your personal decisions to a vote.

Embrace the Struggle

Lots of people tell graduates to "follow your passion," but it's borderline insane to think that everything will turn out fine if all you do is chase your dream career. We rarely get what we *wish* for, but we have at least a shot at getting what we strive, work, and fight for. Pick a field where you have a realistic chance of rising, and turn your less realistic passions—such as playing basketball, sailing, performing music, or painting—into hobbies for your free time.

In your work life, try to embrace your struggles rather than avoiding them. Yes, they may be hard, painful, even terrorizing. But hardships are incredibly formative and educational. They are ultimately the experiences that shape and make careers, and future employers will value your hard-fought struggles. Try to take roles and assignments where the rubber meets the road, where hard but essential problems have to be solved. The further away you get from your company's real action, the slower your career will progress. As time unfolds, you will appreciate the hard times the most.

Make Sure You Never Fear a Reference Check

Nothing puts rocket fuel in your career tank more than what other people say about you. Bosses, peers, and subordinates will all have strong opinions about what you're like to work with. Smart managers know that for anyone well beyond entry level, exhaustive referencing builds a clearer portrait of a candidate than any number of interviews.

Think of everyone around you—bosses, peers, and subordinates—as a potential future reference. What will they say about you? First, of course, whether you get results, move the dial, and make a real impact on your organization. Second, they will say whether you treated everyone, from top to bottom, with respect and consideration. Small kindnesses can be remembered for many years, and you never know if that woman who works down the hall will someday be the hiring manager for a job you really want. This is another aspect of making decisions for the long run.

Career Doldrums and Career Killers

Sometimes your career may get stuck at a certain plateau, no matter how hard you've been working to move up. For good people, career doldrums are usually a function of not being in a growing industry and/or a thriving company. In companies and industries that are dynamic and on the move, people with talent often get promoted even before they are fully ready for a new role. But if you find yourself in the opposite situation, you will have to take the initiative to change your trajectory. I have done so myself on occasion.

First, make sure you're having periodic career check-ins with your direct manager. Good companies and good managers proactively do this because they want to know what's on your mind and how they can hang on to you as an employee. In traditional companies, this kind of conversation happens once a year. In fast-moving companies, it's likely once a quarter. But if you *never* get invited to have a substantive conversation about your career development, that's a red flag. Ask for one.

In these conversations, first reaffirm your commitment to the company and its mission. This signals that you have long-term leadership potential and you're not a mercenary who will jump ship to the highest bidder. Do not be coy or talk about how many calls you've been getting from recruiters; everyone gets those calls. Be constructive, not entitled. The company doesn't owe you a promotion. Employment is a two-way agreement; both sides need to be satisfied with the deal.

There is a school of thought that employees should negotiate hard at every turn to maximize their long-term earnings. I personally never did that, and I didn't need to. I didn't want to have a relationship with my employers that felt purely transactional. But of course there are times when hard bargaining may be essential. You don't want to feel slighted or treated unfairly, which will inevitably lead to you taking calls from recruiters you otherwise would not. Express those sentiments. Employers will listen and respond if they value your retention—and if they don't, that in itself is valuable information. A constructive conversation can do wonders to create a proper, healthy context for your employment and compensation situation.

The factors that may seriously derail or even kill your career are unlikely to be your experience or talent. Most people are, by definition, average performers. It's ultimately about your attitude and behavior, which is a choice, not a skill set. If you don't collaborate well, if you don't take ownership for your project, it won't be long before you're seen as more trouble than you are worth. And this kind of bad behavior is not just an irritant, it reduces your performance and results. Other people will start to avoid working with you on team projects. Before long, your employer will have no choice but to cut you loose. So if you ever get feedback about needing an attitude adjustment, take it seriously.

As I noted earlier in the book, most companies have a mix of passengers and drivers, and sooner or later the passengers get in trouble. During layoffs, they get cut without anyone missing a beat. It doesn't matter how smart you can sound in meetings or how pretty you can make your presentation slides. Ultimately, it's what you can make happen that keeps you in the game. The world eventually catches on to those who mostly manage appearances instead of adding value to the organization.

18

Just for CEOs—Dealing with Founders and Boards

THIS CHAPTER FEATURES two special topics that matter most for CEOs and those who advise them—but it also offers insights for those who are below the CEO level yet aspire to reach it someday.

The Challenge of Succeeding a Founder

There's an ongoing debate about the value of retaining start-up founders as CEOs as their companies grow. In Silicon Valley at least, the pendulum has swung in recent years in favor of founders. Some of the most successful companies in history continued to be led by founders for many years: Bill Gates, Steve Jobs, Marc Benioff, Larry Ellison, Jensen Huang, and so on. But these examples don't account for the many start-ups that were later run into the ground by their founders. So there's no one-size-fits-all solution; some founders make great CEOs, some don't. In general, it's

171

easier to find a start-up founder with good ideas than an operator to execute those ideas to their fullest potential. It's even rarer to find someone who combines both skill sets.

If you are a CEO but not a founder, you may have experienced the discomfort of having to take over from an illustrious trailblazer. I've had to do this several times, as an operator brought in to help each company advance. Some founders have no CEO ambition whatsoever, which makes the transition easier; such was the case for me at Data Domain and Snowflake. Other times, a founder was CEO for a long time and is reluctant to hand over the reins; such was the case for me at ServiceNow.

While I was only employee #22 at Data Domain, the company had been operational for 18 months. Even at that still early stage, I encountered some nostalgia for the early days—before they had sold a single product to a single customer. The lead founder, Dr. Kai Li, was a Princeton computer science professor who had launched a company while on sabbatical but then had to return to teaching. Kai had been acting as chief-cook-and-bottle-washer that first year and a half, keeping everything going. Now the board needed a CEO before fall classes started. The company wasn't failing, but it needed someone who could convert its potential into a thriving business.

ServiceNow, in contrast, had been in business for seven years before I arrived, under the leadership of its founder, Fred Luddy. It already had real revenues, about 250 employees, a solid base of customers, and a trajectory of growth. It was also a San Diego company with a chip on its shoulder about Silicon Valley, the evil empire to the North. It lived and breathed a quirky southern California lifestyle culture, where many staffers went surfing at dawn and wore shorts and flip-flops year-round. They were shocked when I showed up from Silicon Valley with a completely different mindset: pedal to the metal, put your boots on, execution is everything, business is war. You can imagine how well that went over.

Snowflake was a different situation because I wasn't taking over from a founder but from another operator CEO. The company was growing fast and had an exceptional product, so my predecessor, Bob Muglia, was popular among the staff. He held upbeat all-hands meetings every week, plus annual ski trips that took the entire company to Lake Tahoe. What was not to like? But a majority of the board wanted a new CEO who would amp things up. Bob had done a lot of good things to help the company cross the chasm, but now the challenge was to maximize Snowflake's potential after the chasm.

The company was about the same revenue size as ServiceNow when I joined, but it had almost four times as many employees. While ServiceNow had been starving for resources, Snowflake was massively over-resourced. It was a product of its environment: huge amounts of capital raised, unrestrained spending, lots of victory laps, congratulations, and celebrations. My introduction of a much more serious and disciplined approach was like pushing the staff into a cold shower to wake them up.

Tread Lightly as You Make Changes

One key lesson I learned the hard way: Regardless of the situation before you arrived, a non-founder CEO needs to tread lightly at first. The hard part, at least for me, was slowing down my urge to change each culture immediately because I felt enormous pressure to solve problems. After all, the board would never have hired a new CEO unless there were significant issues to be dealt with. The challenge is getting your arms around those issues without throwing the founders under the bus.

First, realize that you're not a founder, and you will never be. Many employees will view you as an interloper, at least at first. The founders may have achieved near-mythical status by what they already accomplished, so what exactly warrants your presence here? The longest-serving employees tend to be the most prone to nostalgia, constantly reliving the romance of the early days. Those days always seem better in retrospect than they did at the time.

Always speak and act with deference toward the founders. You are there to help them realize the promise of their original vision. As CEO, you will eventually get plenty of credit as well as blame, but keep the founders on a pedestal. They earned it, and they belong there. Some founders have a real emotional need for that kind of ongoing recognition, if not adulation, from employees and customers. The company is still their baby, even after they've shifted to an advisory role or a board seat. Even if you're dealing with founders who aren't ego-driven, recognize them anyway. It will help the employees understand that you appreciate the founders—and that you yourself aren't on an ego-driven power trip.

If you manage this delicate balance and the founders speak of you with admiration, that will give you a huge advantage. Start-up boards tend to be dominated by venture capitalists, who can easily get unnerved by whatever their founders are saying about a new CEO. VCs care about their brand image within the community of founders, but much less so among operating executives. VCs see successful founders as rare and precious, to be backed again and again, but they see CEOs as far more replaceable. Especially in technology, CEOs are plow horses while founders are racehorses—so the opinions of your founders will continue to carry weight.

In the Long Run, Success Trumps Popularity

In my early days at several companies, founders openly regretted my hiring and complained to the board behind my back. I was a shock to their system. But when companies succeed massively, as ours all did, even the most disgruntled founders will eventually get over it. Yes, it's nice if they love you, but you can't let yourself get rattled if they don't. Your mission is to win, not to achieve popularity. When you win, paradoxically, you will gain popularity with everybody. But if you get distracted because the founders don't love you, and the company suffers, you will face dark days indeed.

Dan Warmenhoven, the highly successful CEO of NetApp, once remarked that every great CEO has a large ego because you simply could not do this kind of work any other way—but if you can't keep that ego in check, you'll be insufferable and therefore ineffective. That's an uneasy balance.

In the fullness of time, the challenge of managing the sensitivities of the founders will get easier. For example, at all three companies where I was CEO, we grew so fast that it took only a few quarters before the majority of employees no longer predated me. They were all hired after I had taken the helm, which meant they had no prior era to feel nostalgic about.

Even so, continue to share credit as much as possible with the founders. Never lose sight of the fact that success takes a village, and the founders are still honorary members of the village.

The Delicate Art of Board Dynamics

Like founders, the members of your board of directors also require skillful relationship building and boundary setting.

The role of the board is often a source of confusion for new CEOs. It's unclear where their purview ends and management's responsibilities start. In a perfect world, board members would always respect a clear boundary between giving the CEO advice and support, versus trying to tell the CEO how to run the company. But in practice, the dividing line is often a blur. Board members often can't resist overreaching into management territory. Less seasoned CEOs allow them to cross that line because the board hired them, so they feel like the board members are their bosses.

But the relationship isn't that simple. Of course it's true that one role of the board is to hire and fire the CEO. But short of removal for serious offenses, a good board will give the CEO near-total authority over strategy and operations. And it will treat removing the CEO as a gut-wrenching, high-risk, last-resort move, never to be done casually or for frivolous reasons. Hiring a new one is a lengthy process and sets up a potentially damaging short-term leadership void. So good boards prefer not to go there.

On the other hand, most board members have held powerful roles in the past and may be aching for opportunities to assert themselves. They want to stay relevant, a very understandable human emotion. This is especially true for VC board members, who often have the benefit of extensive exposure to a variety of companies, after serving on many different boards. On top of that, VC investors on your board will consider it "their money" you're spending, which they feel gives them even more justification to cross the line. That's another very understandable human emotion and another reason that board dynamics can become extremely tricky.

Don't get me wrong; I'm not suggesting that you tell board members to take a flying leap and dismiss their feedback out of hand. They are there to enrich the conversation, ask critical questions, offer fresh perspectives, and make sure the interests of investors are well considered. All of that is helpful and productive and can increase everyone's confidence in the company's direction. The problems only start when the board crosses the line and tries to force the CEO's hand.

What Not to Do: Subservience

New CEOs often hesitate to assert their purview because they aren't sure where and how the boundaries should be drawn. It's only human in that situation to try to please and appease those loud and intimidating voices. I urge you to suppress that reflex. Since nature abhors a vacuum, if you are subservient, there will be no shortage of board members who will gladly jump in and start bossing you around.

Especially with new CEOs, boards often try to establish a probationary period, when the CEO has to check in frequently. But if they treat you like a teenager with a curfew, how will they know when you're ready to act independently? They may find excuses to keep that probationary dynamic going indefinitely if you seem fine with it.

Some CEOs are naturally compliant and reflexively seek consensus with the board, right or wrong. They take a measure of comfort because a decision made by the board isn't as scary; they aren't alone or out on a limb. While that comfort may be soothing in the short run, it won't help you keep your job. Conceding the board's authority for every major decision isn't playing it safe. In fact, in the long run it's much riskier than asserting your own authority and legitimacy and taking responsibility for your own decisions.

I sometimes wonder what goes on in the boardrooms of large, household name institutions that have gone sideways and struggled for decades. Their leadership is usually politically correct, with quotes in their press releases that will make you yawn, and they never do or say anything anyone might disagree with. Yet their revenues decline year in and year out. They use their cash to buy back stock. Their acquisitions are mired in the past, not skating to where the puck is going to be.

Those board members may sleep soundly, but they shouldn't. And CEOs who "go along to get along" with that kind of board shouldn't sleep soundly either. Sooner or later, activist investors will rebel, overhaul the board, and kick a board-compliant CEO to the curb. There are no safe harbors; you have to get comfortable being uncomfortable.

Another problem with board-compliant CEOs is that they lose their leadership mojo with the rank and file. When employees hear that a CEO's plan was thwarted by the board, they wonder who is really running the company. The same is true if the CEO starts every statement about strategy with, "The board wants us to. . . ."

You're not there to make friends or get a gold star for obeying orders; you are there to win. The board will sing your praises to the skies if the company hits all its targets under your leadership, even if you disregard their suggestions. Conversely, if the company struggles, members of the board will blame you and maybe eventually cut you loose. When that unpleasant moment arrives, it won't matter how many board dinners you attended, how much you've flattered them, or even if you've followed all their wishes against your own better judgment.

What to Do Instead: Lead Your Board

CEOs rarely push anywhere near the limits of their true power as commander in chief. Whether you feel ready or not, once you have the big job you might as well act like it. A good CEO will *lead* a board.

What does that mean? For starters, never go into a board meeting, tee up a topic, and ask them what they think. Instead, prep carefully with your team in advance, and then go in and tell them what *you* think. If they then respond with questions or concerns, that's fine. You have started the meeting by filling a vacuum, instead of creating one. That will make it much harder for them to dominate the discussion.

Preparation is your key advantage. You have been thinking about the topic at hand for days or weeks, while most board members are probably coming in cold. They typically come to a board meeting four times a year; how much do they really know about what's going on? Their gut instincts can't compete with your data, analysis, and careful planning. Their operational biases, based on their own unique histories and experiences, should therefore be taken with a large pinch of salt. So figure out the right answers in advance, and then lead the board to form a consensus with you, rather than offering to form one with them.

Even if you get good at leading your board, there may be times when they feel strongly about the substance of an issue that should fall on the CEO's side of the boundary line. For instance, I have seen board compensation committees try to tie CEO compensation to compliance with the board's direction on strategy. A CEO should never surrender such an important topic.

Similarly, a compensation committee's charter normally focuses on compensation for executives who report directly to the CEO. This is appropriate because the CEO is the only one who doesn't have a boss, and oversight is necessary for good governance. But even then, the CEO must have a strong say in the compensation of his or her top executives. The board can make sure everything is well aligned and within reasonable boundaries for the industry, but in general the CEO should make the case for appropriate compensation for each senior exec.

When some board members insisted on controlling a decision that fell on my side of the boundary, I have occasionally told them that they will have to find a new CEO if they want to overrule me on such matters. That's a dramatic tactic, not to be used lightly, but keep it in your back pocket if you ever need to prove that you're serious about defending the purview of your role. CEOs can't be too wedded to their jobs and must be willing to put their badge on the line when necessary. You might never find it necessary to issue that ultimatum, and even if you do, you may not need to follow through. But you must be mentally prepared to walk away to preserve your scope of authority as CEO, or your tenure in office will be irreparably compromised.

Good CEOs get comfortable asserting their authority. They've got plenty of it under the structures and customs of corporate life. Use it or lose it.

19

Conclusion—Great Leaders Have Great Outcomes

I AM ASKED on occasion what makes a great CEO. People expect a series of adjectives such as intelligent, charismatic, collaborative, eloquent, and so on. Something they can scribble on a sticky note and put up on their bathroom mirror for daily inspiration. Of course the answer isn't so simple, as I'm sure you now realize as we conclude this guide for current and future CEOs.

There are many different paths to superior outcomes in business. You will have to find your own path, one that suits your temperament, disposition, and natural aptitudes. Therefore, don't try to copy or emulate other leaders—including me. Don't ask yourself in tough situations, "What would Frank do?" That will only slow down the process of finding your own path.

Instead, make the most of your unique aggregate of experiences. Apply those experiences, and the insights we've discussed in previous chapters, to become a truer, more honed, more effective version of who you already are. Finding your own path, however long it takes, will unlock your personal power.

I've known many young CEOs who have all the prerequisites on paper: they're smart, energetic, hard-working, ambitious. But then they get handed a big leadership role before they've had the necessary experiences to discover their own path. As a result, they often get bruised and bloodied. As hard as it can be to suffer the indignity of failure, those bad experiences later become the bedrock of their future success.

Only in hindsight will you truly realize what your experiences have meant. That is why it's okay to embrace your inevitable challenges and setbacks as part of your journey. They are there for a reason.

At the end of the day, great leaders at any level have great outcomes. You can be the most empathetic, charismatic, and popular leader ever, but none of that will matter if your business falls short. And when it does, there will be nowhere for you to hide. No one will care about your legitimate explanations, let alone your excuses. No one will care about the unlucky breaks that were completely beyond your control. Is that fair? Of course not! But it's the world we live in, the world we have to accept as leaders.

The good news is that if you persevere over long periods of time, if you focus intensely on delivering value for customers, and if you build a disciplined culture for your employees, it will all pay off in the long run. You will drive great outcomes for your organization and reap the rewards. It's hard to beat any leader who combines great resolve, persistence, mission focus, and clarity about what is and is not important.

It's hard to beat any leader who truly amps it up.

My very best wishes to you as you continue your leadership journey.

Acknowledgments

I WOULD LIKE to express my gratitude and appreciation for all the people and institutions that have had a profound effect on my life and trajectory, and my special thanks to everyone who helped and encouraged me to write this book.

To my wife, Brenda, who always encouraged me to not hold back and take chances and risks when it wasn't so obvious—notably during our return to the Netherlands 25 years ago, which was so formative for what was to come.

To all the employees, managers, and executives at Data Domain, ServiceNow, and Snowflake, who came together day in and day out to deliver the outstanding experiences we had at these companies over a period of two decades. Our work together was not just instructive and productive; we thoroughly enjoyed the ride every day, as it was happening.

To Denise Persson, chief marketing officer at Snowflake, who wanted this book written and orchestrated the effort so I could keep doing my day job as well.

To Will Weisser, who structured and made sense of my narratives and ideas, turning them into a real, publishable book.

To Mike Campbell at Wiley, who saw something in the idea of publishing these thoughts and observations.

To all my venture capital friends, who kept pestering me for years about writing another book.

It is hard to overstate the influence my alma mater, Erasmus University Rotterdam, had on me. The university environment in the broadest sense directly influenced my focus, outlook, and ambition as an adolescent. It also led to my eventual move to the United States.

Speaking of which, I would be remiss to not acknowledge my adopted home country of the United States. A career like mine can only happen in America, period, and I thank my good fortune for wandering over here as a young man.

Frank Slootman
Ennis, Montana
August 2021

Index

Also available: *The Amp It Up Fieldbook*

Hyper scale your organization with practical prompts and exercises

Building on Slootman's ideas presented in *Amp It Up* along with his personal experience over three decades of building hyper-growth companies, this fieldbook helps readers easily apply his conceptual first principles, mindsets, and tactical advice to their own organizations and careers.

Readers will learn about:

- How to align people around first principles that guide change and execute with urgency and intensity every day
- Maximizing growth and scale without making expensive changes to talent, structure, or fundamental business models
- The three essential characteristics of great mission statements, and why Slootman chose Snowflake's current mission statement, broken down word-by-word
- How to identify personal blind spots that keep us from achieving our best